Time to Love
Celebrating Ninety

Mary White

Memoir
ISBN 978-0-9930522-0-0

9 780993 052200

First published in 2014

Typeset by GreenGate Publishing Services, Tonbridge, Kent
Printed in Glasgow by Bell & Bain Ltd

Cover: 'Norfolk Lilies', original watercolour by Mary White

Acknowledgement

Especial thanks go to Jay, my husband, who has with patient care helped me to become 'computer literate', edited my manuscript and coordinated the photographs.

Dedication

To my husband, Jay, and to my family present and beyond.

List of photographs

Contents

Preface

Life is a gift and the living of it is a lifetime's learning experience. From being nurtured by our mothers we make choices and decisions which influence the way we live our lives. The golden thread is learning to love, the hardest lesson of all, but the only one to give us the happiness for which we all strive, and when this happens it is a celebration.

Chapter one

Home and away

*Let us celebrate the way we were and the
way we live now*

Let us celebrate the way we will be

From the foreword by Roger McGough in
Poems of Celebration

I am ninety years of age and my reason for writing
this autobiographical memoir is the realisation of the
importance of being positive and loving. It is a privilege
to have the time and opportunity to make things right.

I am fortunate in being married to the most wonderful
man for the last fourteen years. I met him at
watercolour class. I realise that the 'me' he loves has
been honed and polished through the years. And here
is my story.

I was born Joan Mary Huson on 20th February 1924.
My mother, Emily (Em) was a vivid personality inherited
from her Welsh father. My father, Charles (Charlie),
was a typical Norfolk man, strong, solid, loyal, with a
sense of humour and jokes told with a straight face.

Home and away

He instilled in me a pride of being born in Norfolk. One day, to my amazement, he started singing in his rich bass voice an eight verse Norfolk ballad. I remember the refrain which went like this:

She's fat and she's beautiful

She's fat and she's fair

She's just like them buttercups

A blooming down there.

My mother would accompany him on the piano, and my father would sing 'Excelsior' and 'Tom of Devon'.

My father was an ironmonger in a shop founded by my grandfather.

I loved the smell of my father's shop. It was musty and smelling of brushes, freshly chopped wood and briquettes which were made of coal dust. The counter was solid, looking like half a tree trunk, black and smooth. As the shop was nearly one hundred years old the counter could have been half a tree. Behind the counter was a raft of small drawers containing screws, nails and mysterious substances. My father knew unerringly the whereabouts of every item. There was a huge tank of paraffin beside the counter and the tank was filled up about every two weeks by an enormous tanker. The Valor paraffin burning heaters were very popular and inexpensive. Customers brought their two gallon cans to be filled up by the two gallon measurer kept by the tank or my father delivered it, putting the filled cans in a box on his bike. He was very strong and delivered the paraffin in all weathers, leaving my mother to serve in the shop which was very inconvenient when she was cooking. Large sheets of tin stood along the wall leading to the long workshop, where my father mended kettles and saucepans. He would shake the sheet of tin to make it sound like thunder to amuse me. He would take a large roll of wire netting to the pavement outside and cut it to the required length with a huge pair of shears. I still love the smell of the ironmongers shop.

The best thing about the shop was the fact that he sold fireworks. A large glass case of them would appear and I was allowed to chose my favourite rockets which sprayed golden rain.

My father had frequent attacks of tonsillitis and, although he was in his forties, was advised to have his tonsils removed. When he awoke after the operation he was astonished to find that his chest was very painful. The surgeon told him that he had stopped breathing on the operating table and that they had to perform artificial respiration. He was in hospital for four days and on the fifth was home and in the shop. He was a real stoic.

We never had a holiday until I was in my teens. Early on, shops were open until ten o'clock at night. Then the shops closed at six o'clock with a half day on Thursdays. The shop was always shut on bank holidays when we would go on a day trip to Gorleston. We took the train to Yarmouth and then the ferry to Gorleston. One day at Yarmouth there were rows and rows of trestle tables by the harbour with Scottish fishergirls gutting herrings and throwing them into barrels. They travelled along the coast from fishing port to fishing port gutting the herrings.

When the war came of course no one had a holiday.

Although I lived in London for fifty years my roots are in Norfolk where I visit every year. My parents were miss-matched but they both loved me. I was breast fed and nurtured and the only child. Therefore the foundations were laid for being the person I am.

Christmas at my paternal grandfather's was a traditional family affair with a turkey dinner served under the softly hissing gas lamps. The drawing room was also gas lit with oil paintings of my grandparents looking down on us. My favourite Auntie Kitty who was also my godmother played the piano while we sang carols. She had curvature of the spine (scoliosis) and in spite of many treatments from the osteopath her curvature never lessened. When the children were told that Father Christmas (my uncle) was coming up the garden path with a linen basket full of presents we rushed to the window to watch. The excitement mounted as he knocked on the door. One year I was overwhelmed with presents and I said 'I do not want any more Father Christmas'.

Home and away

My grandfather with his bald head, white beard and large brass ear trumpet was quite a character. He kept a red and grey parrot in a cage on the breakfast room table. One day Polly escaped and the fire service was called because she was espied in a high tree on the main Newmarket Road. My grandfather died when I was nine and my Auntie Kitty stayed on in the large lonely gas lit house. My aunt never married and was often not at home, visiting numerous relatives and keeping house when various babies were born. Everyone loved Auntie Kitty and I knew that she loved me, and I would often spend a day with Auntie Kitty watching her take the wholemeal bread out of the bread oven on the wall. Her bread won first prize at the Norwich Ideal Homes Exhibition. I loved to watch my aunt doing the ironing with the flaring gas iron, and I would help her light the dining room fire working the bellows and singing:

Blow the fire blacksmith,
Blow the fire Jack.
Blow the fire my little old man,
And see the fire crack.

Sometimes I stayed the night, sinking deep into the soft feather bed, the room being lit by an oil lamp or candle. Auntie Kitty made toffee apples and fudge which she knocked out with a small hammer. She was wonderful with my friends telling us that the three foot high stone in the garden was a growing stone. We would solemnly sit on the stone to see if it had grown.

When I was eleven we moved from our small terraced house to a house next door to the shop. I was sent with my friend to tear the wallpaper off the walls and we had a hilarious time. Our garden adjoined my grandfather's garden and was a wonderful play area.

On some Sundays we visited my grandfather's sister, my very small Aunt Emma, and tall muscular be-whiskered Uncle Tom. Aunt Emma was always dressed in a long black dress and a bonnet out of doors. We would pass the monkey puzzle tree and be ushered into the drawing room where I sat on a horse hair sofa and my bare legs would stick to the surface and had to be carefully peeled away. I was fascinated by the moving balls of the ormolu clock on the mantelpiece, on either side of which were magnificent vases depicting a goose girl and her flock. We had tea in the dark dining room and I remember bone jelly (ugh!) and delicious lemon buns. After tea we tramped down to the cool whitewashed cellar where the food was kept.

When Aunt Emma died it was discovered that she had worn winceyette knee level drawers with a convenient slit at the crutch. She also wore red flannel petticoats under her long black skirts. She had pink bows on her brass bed knobs and her chamber pot was kept on a lace doily.

Home and away

My mother was keen that I should have a good education. My father was not a good businessman and his inheritance was absorbed in the shop to keep it afloat. My mother struggled with the meagre house-keeping money to provide the needs of the home. It was imperative that I passed the eleven plus. I had to win a scholarship. On the walk to school mother asked me intelligence questions and one of her favourite spellings was 'phlegm'. She had been a nurse so spellings were sometimes medical. She was a great storyteller and told stories of her childhood as we walked into the country every Saturday afternoon. I am always moved by Dylan Thomas' 'Poem in October' when he walked with his 'mother through the parables of sunlight and the legends of the green chapels'.

Those walks were the highlights of my week, as we walked along hearing stories of my mother's childhood. My mother was nearly killed by a falling chimney pot; and another time her head was stuck in a farmyard gate; and then there was the time she met the King. She heard that King Edward the Seventh was coming to Melton Constable Station. She saw this large red faced man alight from the train. She went up to him and asked 'Are you the King?' and he said he was. 'Where is your crown?' asked my mother and he explained that he only wore it occasionally and he patted her under the chin. When she told her parents she was told to wash her face thoroughly. My maternal Grandfather was a great inspiration to me. He died before I was born but my mother told me so much about him. He was Welsh, coming from a large mining family in the Rhondda. He locked an old man in a lavatory and because of which he had to leave school at the age of ten. The railways were being built and my grandfather was employed by them eventually becoming Chief Permanent Way Inspector and responsible for overseeing the laying of the railway lines. He was an inventor and among other things he created the train buffers. He played three musical instruments and was an amusing story teller, reducing the family to helpless laughter.

When my mother was young there was very little opportunity for women other than teaching or nursing. My mother's three brothers had been educated at Gresham's Public School at Holt, while the girls attended the village school. In 1915 and at the age of twenty-eight my mother decided to become a nurse. Her only option was training at what was then the hospital for the poor at the workhouse. It was a hard training with one free day a month and a yearly week's holiday. The salary was five pounds per annum for the first year, ten pounds for the second year and finally fifteen pounds. She was often the only nurse on duty at night in a ward of forty men. However, she bravely stayed the course and qualified as a State Registered Nurse and joined the College of Nursing Ltd. She was given a silver badge with her qualified number engraved on the back. The Royal College of Nursing was still to be founded. She became a 'Private' nurse for four years going into the homes of the privileged, wearing her cloak and flowing veil. Mother said that moths were often caught in her veil when she was on night duty. I loved playing nurses in my mother's uniform. Her cloak was made into my school gym tunic!

My mother. Student nurse, 1915

My father was silent at home and jovial in the shop. My parents tolerated one another. I do not remember expressions of love from my father either to myself or my mother. I attended a Congregational Church three times on Sundays. My father had a good bass voice and sang in the excellent choir. I came to appreciate the sermons preached with passion and having a good exegesis by a succession of Welsh ministers.

I enjoyed learning but was bullied at the Church of England Primary school in College Road where Edith

Home and away

Cavell had lived. Edith Cavell was a vicar's daughter born in a village just outside Norwich. She is buried by the walls of Norwich Cathedral and my mother went to her funeral. I always remember her words 'Patriotism is not enough I must have no hatred in my heart for anyone'. She was a very brave and dedicated woman who saved the life of at least two hundred soldiers in the First World War and was executed by the Germans for helping the prisoners to escape.

The College School was an excellent school attached to a teacher training college and I with two others won a place at the Girl's Public Day School Trust (G.P.D.S.T.) Norwich High School. I remember my father presenting me with my first watch as he gave me my morning tea, and told me of my success. I always felt under pressure as I was a 'scholarship' girl and had to succeed. New subjects were always looming such as French, Latin, Geometry, Algebra, Chemistry and Physics. We had to buy all our books which was an expense, as well as all my attractive green uniform and this included six pairs of shoes. However, we did not have to carry books home at night which children have to do these days except those for our homework.

I was fifteen in 1939 when war was declared. We were told that a French politician would be visiting us and we were all to sing the Marsellaise, and then shout with enthusiasm 'Vive la France, Vive l'Angleterre'. We were so disappointed when he did not arrive.

Home and away

When I sat the Oxford and Cambridge Joint Certificate examinations they were interrupted by bombing and air raid sirens. We would sit in the sand-bagged cloak-rooms singing 'One man went to mow a meadow' as we were not allowed to talk.

I left school at sixteen after mother had seen the headmistress to discuss subjects that I could take in the sixth form, which would be helpful to my nursing ambitions.

It was decided that a job 'in the real world' would be a better preparation. I was bitterly disappointed when I was sent to secretarial college to learn shorthand and typing. I wanted to be a nurse, not a secretary, and to my everlasting regret refused to learn shorthand which would have been so useful during my nursing lectures.

After five months I was accepted as a filing clerk in the Inland Revenue Office.

I felt that my education had been in vain with this boring job but mother was pleased because I was working for the Civil Service in a nice safe job with a good salary! However, the hours were long starting at 8.30am and finishing at 6pm and working Saturday mornings. There was also fire watching, which meant staying until 10pm one evening a week. We were shown how to use a stirrup pump, in case of incendiary bombs, which was never needed in spite of frequent raids. One night there was a thick fog, a real 'pea souper'. Traffic was at a

standstill and I was cautiously finding my way when
I heard my father's family Huson whistle. I whistled in
return and we found one another. Thank goodness
those fogs are no more. I remember newborn babies
with throaty coughs and cleaning the fog dirty tiles of
the labour ward. Many people died of fog related chest
infections. The Clean Air Act limited the use of coal-
burning fires whose smoke caused the smog.

When I was seventeen, Norwich had a week of severe
bombing raids. One night the siren went and my
father quickly donned his Air Raid Warden's uniform
and my mother and I dashed to our Anderson shelter.
I heard the bomb descending which landed nearby
demolishing our shop and house and my grandfather's
house. All was silent and I thought everyone was dead
and then I heard my father's voice 'Are you all right?'.
It was so wonderful. He was alive. As we walked to
where Auntie Kitty was staying I was unaware that
my stockings were trailing over my slippers. It was like
walking in a dream or nightmare. My father, in his tin
hat and navy blue uniform, had tears streaming down
his face. I was so thankful that we were all alive, and
I said 'Don't cry Pop, we are alive!'. It never occurred
to me until years later what had happened to our
neighbours. Recently, in a Norwich museum we saw
that over two hundred people had been killed on that
night. This devastating tragedy made me realise that
people are more important than possessions. I am
always content and appreciative of what I have and this
insight has been so helpful. My father erected a huge

Union Jack on his ruined shop of which the only thing remaining was his safe with the doors cracked from the heat, but the deeds of his shop and house were intact.

My parents, 1943

My parents were lent a house by a member of our church, and my father was given a job in a large ironmongers. They had lost their glasses, their dentures and all their clothes apart from those they were wearing. My mother had small feet and stuffed cotton wool into shoes so that she could walk. The next day we obtained clothing coupons and went shopping for clothes. My parents had to wait six weeks for their dentures which was very difficult for them as they could only eat soft food, but I do not remember them complaining. Eventually it was found that the pantry under the stairs was intact and precious china was rescued. Some of my books were retrieved but my stamps and letters from my South African relatives were lost. I still have books with their covers stained by water. The strength of the stairs had also saved my mother's piano which was able to be cleaned and retuned.

People were so kind, especially the two members of our church whom we hardly knew who lent us their house for two years. It was modern, near the country and my mother would get on her borrowed bike to gather mushrooms for breakfast. I also remember a large dustbin in the road where food waste was collected to feed the pigs. My father continued fire watching making new relationships at the A.R.P. post. He also had a job at a large hardware shop in the city.

The bombing had a life-changing effect on me. I felt that I needed to get on with my life and I applied to University College Hospital (U.C.H.) to be a student nurse. There was a two year waiting list and I was not accepted until 1st April 1943, when I was nineteen and the Routledge Report became law, ending the need to pay for nurse training. London was subject to rockets and doodlebugs, and was still a dangerous place. However, my parents were completely supportive of my decision to train as a nurse. That is love!

There were thirty-two in our set, Set 73, and we were housed in the large nurses' home in Huntley Street. On our first evening we were told to take a toothbrush with our nurses caps to the classroom. We had to wet the tape in the cap so that we could draw it up to the required pleated shape. We had six weeks in the preliminary training school, having lectures and learning nursing procedures. Nothing prepared me for the reality of nursing. My first ward was a twenty-eight bedded mens' medical ward and I was very shy. The men would whistle marching tunes to encourage me to walk in step as I passed with bottles or bedpans. I was forever blushing and they called me Rosie. We were on duty from eight in the morning until eight in the evening, with two hours free time in the day, and one day off in the week. I had blisters on the soles of my feet and I slept with the foot of my bed raised on a chair. However, we made friends and supported one another. The food was very bad and we were always hungry. We carried our rations with us in a bag called a 'pinch' bag but there was nothing to pinch! My mother would send me a cake every month. She was able to do this with the contents of the South African food parcels from our relatives. They sent us plump raisins, sugar and delicious tinned fruit.

We were very fortunate because one of the nurses in our set was a farmer's daughter from Bude. Her parents would send large bacon and egg pies and strawberries and cream, which she would generously share and which we would eat out of soap dishes using tooth brushes as spoons.

Home and away

After three months on day duty I was sent to a women's surgical ward for night duty. Night duty was twelve nights on and four nights off. There were two of us on duty. As the junior nurse I was responsible for cleaning the sluice and for washing bowls and bedpans. The staff nurse sterilised the instruments and packed the sterilising drums with dressings ready to be autoclaved. The patients were encouraged to make the dressings. There were also treatments to be carried out and when we were 'on the door' we had to receive emergencies. If I had to go to theatre with the patient for an operation the senior nurse was left on her own. On returning to the ward I would sit with the patient until she had recovered consciousness and was stable, monitoring the pulse and blood pressure every fifteen minutes. We were always very busy.

One night a doodlebug fell in Tottenham Court Road and one of those seriously injured was Rose, a red headed cockney. She had lost her entire family and eventually had her leg amputated. Her bed was situated behind Sister's desk and she never appeared to sleep. She drank endless cups of tea, and I was forever retrieving her full bedpans and she would say 'Take it away Ramsbottom'. She was an inspiration to us all. She was so brave. Although we worked hard, I loved the patients on that ward and still remember them. Another night when I was on a men's medical ward a raging fire broke out at Maples' mattress factory. If the fire threatened the hospital we were instructed to move the patients on to blankets and drag them to the lift. Thankfully the fire was dealt with and was under control.

We cooked breakfast for twenty-eight patients and at the midnight meal would discuss our breakfast recipes. The dried egg would be scrambled in the porringer; we would put the bacon on a tray in a low oven at 4.30am; and the boiled eggs were tied up in muslin and plunged into boiling water for the required time. To our relief, sometimes it was pilchards which we did not have to cook. Patients would help with the early morning tea and porridge. We would have to complete ten blanket baths and make the beds before the day staff arrived at 8am and the report was read.

Nursing was very different from my early fantasies. I loved the patients but I was scared of the daily challenges most of the time. Fifty years later we had a nurse's reunion and every one agreed that they were also scared but we all smiled.

It was so important for me to leave home and become independent especially as I was an only child. I was fortunate in choosing one of the best hospitals in the world. I was influenced by my mother whose matron was trained at U.C.H. Antibiotics were undiscovered and washing hands and cleaning were a priority. I think it was in 1947 when penicillin was first used intravenously and then by four-hourly injections. When I cared for a nurse with diphtheria penicillin nasal drops were used. Streptomycin was a breakthrough in the treatment of T.B. An old school friend of mine languishing in a sanatorium for five months was able to return home because of the new treatment.

Poliomyelitis vaccine was not yet available, and three nurses were paralysed to various degrees, one being unable to walk. Children with whooping cough were admitted to a unit where they had special treatment for their collapsed lungs and other chest problems.

However, to return to my own story. At the end of my first year I was home on holiday when I developed an abscess under my arm. I was admitted to the Norfolk and Norwich Hospital for treatment. I was a patient for five weeks as, of course, there were no antibiotics. It was a valuable learning curve being a patient and I also realised how fortunate I was at being trained at U.C.H.

There were wonderful plays in London, especially at Wyndham's Theatre which featured Laurence Olivier and Ralph Richardson, and also the famous Sybil Thorndike. We were sometimes fortunate in obtaining complimentary tickets and there was also a kiosk in Trafalgar Square where theatre tickets were sometimes available. If I were early enough I could put a stool outside Wyndham's Theatre to secure a one and sixpenny seat in the 'gods'. One night at Wyndham's there were two plays. One featured Laurence Olivier as the tragic Oedipus in which it is horrific when he dashes out his eyes, and the other a light hearted Sheridan play in which Laurence Oliver rode down on the theatre curtain. All for one and sixpence. I remember having a complimentary ticket for the second row of the stalls at Covent Garden and watching Moira Shearer dancing in 'Red Shoes'. The roads were dark, the lights were dimmed and there was very little traffic so that I felt safer walking in the road on the way home. Voices could be heard and often they were American and people would emerge out of the gloom. We had to sign out and sign in and had to be back by 10.30pm.

Travelling home to Norwich was difficult. Warren Street underground station platforms were a nightly dormitory for those wanting a safe night's sleep. The train to Norwich was always crowded, often with airmen and the acrid smell of their uniform pervaded. There was often only standing room and the dimmed lights meant reading was impossible. Also, the trains were often late but my father was always there at the barrier to meet me. I was always thrilled to be home. I so missed the green fields and the cosiness of home but I never told my parents of my homesickness.

I was often alone on my day off as quite often my friend was on the same ward and could not have a day off at the same time. I would go to the Lyons Corner House at the corner of Tottenham Court Road and Oxford Street for breakfast, first buying *The Times* newspaper. I would order breakfast from the waitress or 'nippy', smartly dressed with traditional white apron and cap.

Porridge was hot, creamy and delicious. There was very little choice so I would often have tomatoes on toast accompanied by toast and marmalade and a pot of tea.

I was always hungry and would think of food at home before the war. I would think of warming my knees in front of the fire in the sitting room, and making toast with our long brass toasting fork. If it was a Monday, spreading toast with the dripping from the Sunday joint. Mother made delicious light Norfolk dumplings, the size of a grapefruit, made with only flour and water to have with gravy before the main meat course. Then, there was 'pig's fry' which was pig's offal bought from the pork butcher. It mainly consisted of liver and sweetbreads. Mother would cook it in a roasting tin with sage and onion gravy and a crispy large dumpling in the middle. It was a succulent meal and one of my favourites. Suet puddings were an especial delight with apple pudding and mincemeat roly poly boiled in a cloth in a large saucepan. Mother used to recount the fact that their school puddings were boiled in the clothes' copper!

I must return to my day off. I would walk to the comprehensive bookshop, Foyles, in Charing Cross Road where I would happily browse until I went to the National Gallery where I would often join a lecture. I would then go to the basement for a sandwich and a coffee. Hatchards bookshop in Piccadilly was another favourite place. Bond Street with Yardley's and Coty was a source of luxurious soap at times, and was worth a visit. Soap was rationed so this was such a treat and good for presents. My salary was just over three pounds a month so I would return to U.C.H. for dinner.

However, in 1945 the darkness lifted. On V.E. Day a group of us gravitated to Buckingham Palace where we were soon separated in the enormous joyous crowds. The war was over at last. 'We want the King' was chanted and then we were ecstatic when the Royal Family appeared on the balcony. Then we surged to Whitehall where Churchhill stood on a balcony with his wispy hair blowing in the wind. He said 'Now we shall sing Rule Britannia' and starting on a flat note we all stood there singing 'Wule Bwittania', as he had said with his customary impediment. I shall never forget how euphoric we were, with strangers embracing strangers and men climbing lamp posts. It was such a relief after all the dark days.

The nurse training was for four years and in my last year I was asked whether there was a procedure that I would like to witness and I chose seeing a baby born. When I saw the ease with which the baby was delivered and the joy on the mother's face I knew that I wanted to be a midwife. I wrote to Queen Mary's Maternity Home and was accepted as a pupil midwife for the six month's training.

Chapter two
New life and new babies

I see you dart into the world
Transformation by Jeni Couzyn

Queen Mary's Maternity Home was unique. It was
so different from the built-up area around U.C.H. and
Tottenham Court Road. It was near Hampstead Heath
and had spacious gardens. The building was designed
by Lutyens and built on a hill in Hampstead. Keats had
played bowls on our lawn. It had been founded by
Queen Mary for First World War ex-servicemen's wives.
The first floor was for the wives and the ground floor
was for their small children and called 'Toddlers'. The
antenatal clinic was in the spacious gardens. The staff
bedrooms were on the second floor with its attractive
dormer windows. The atmosphere was so different
from U.C.H. It was about new life instead of disease,
and was one of happy expectancy and the joy of new
birth.

Miss Lois Beaulah, the Matron, had trained at U.C.H.
and had been on the midwifery 'flying squad' called to
difficult home births. She was an outstanding lecturer,
inspired confidence and on my eighth delivery handed

me a large curved needle, already threaded, and taught me to suture the torn perineum.

There were about ten student midwives, all from London teaching hospitals – mainly Guy's, U.C.H., The London and Westminster, now called Charing Cross Hospital. Westminster Hospital was planned on separate floors, each floor having its own consultant, accident and emergency wards, and theatres like a cottage hospital. The students from Wesminster always seemed to be happy and also very efficient. We had time off for lectures, experience in the art of delivering babies and learnt every aspect of being a midwife before we took part one of the midwifery certificate. This did not qualify one to be a midwife, which required another six months practical training.

There were relaxation classes for the mothers and also a fathers' class. Husbands sat with their wives until it was time for delivery so father's classes were important.

However, some of our patients were from a nearby home for unmarried mothers who were referred to Queen Mary's by the Moral Welfare Officer. (It was a sin to have an illegitimate baby). The single mothers attended the antenatal clinic for the last six weeks of their pregnancy, whilst they lived at the home for unmarried mothers, which they kept scrupuously clean. When they went into labour they were never on their own but they always had a pupil midwife in attendance because they were often tense and frightened. They had to breast feed their babies for six weeks at which point their babies were adopted. It was a heartbreaking situation.

Queen Mary visited every year and provided the pink and blue cot shawls. She also designed bed jackets which were not used and were carefully kept in mothballs until she visited. Three exquisite layettes were given to the babies born or near Queen Mary's birthday and made by her Sewing Guild in Canada. A baby party was held each year when these babies were about a year old. The weather always seemed to be fine and it was such a delight to see the babies on mattresses on the lawns under the trees. At one visit Queen Mary asked Matron if the post-natal mothers wore binders and was told that they did exercises whereupon Queen Mary replied 'I wore binders with all my six children and look at my good figure!'.

Another good thing was the food which was both plentiful and delicious and eaten in an attractive dining room with its round oak tables overlooking the garden. I was no longer hungry.

Sometimes we would pass the Vale of Health and climb over the gate of Kenwood Park to watch the owls emerging from the trees. I thought of Keats who lived just down the road writing 'Ode to a Nightingale' which he was supposed to have composed on Hampstead Heath. The Vale of Health was so called because in the nineteenth century when there was a cholera epidemic in London those living in the Vale of Health, drinking clean water, were unaffected. Therefore, it was realised that cholera lived in water and the epidemic had started from the Aldgate pump. This was the beginning of the huge task of providing clean water for all.

The post-natal mothers were usually discharged at ten days and for the last three days they lived in 'Toddlers' which was converted into accommodation for mothers to care for their babies prior to going home. Patients staying in longer meant better and more enjoyable relationships with the nurses.

I left Queen Mary's after six months to take the second part of my midwifery training which was home births or 'on the district', as it was called. I chose to go to Norwich, my home city, to train. There were six of us each assigned to a certain district and mine was a new housing estate.

On two consecutive mornings I passed the same policeman on my bike at 5am. He said 'Can't you sleep?'. My bag of equipment was strapped on the back of the bike and in my front basket were two nitrous oxide cylinders. Negotiating corners was a bit hazardous as the cylinders clanked from side to side changing my balance. I loved delivering babies at home with granny or a neighbour to help, with siblings coming in to greet the new baby. We were overseen by a senior midwife who often did not arrive until the baby was born.

For one delivery I had to send for the doctor as the baby was not advancing. We boiled the forceps on the cooker and I gave the ether anaesthetic. Once when my colleague was off duty I was sent to her case. It was the mother's third child and after delivering the baby it was evident that there was a second baby there. The second baby was much smaller and looked premature. This was a very rare case of two babies conceived at different times, called superfecundation. The babies both thrived but the parents were shocked.

Recently my husband and I went on holiday to Norwich and found to my amazement that the hotel annexe was none other than the house where I had stayed when working on the district.

I chose to train in Norwich especially to see my parents new 'pre-fab'. They were overjoyed. It was their first home of their own after three years of sharing with others. They loved the fitted kitchen complete with a fridge and cooker. The Swedish government had donated furniture and household goods for those who were bombed out. My parents were given a kitchen table, two stools, cutlery, a wardrobe and two single beds. They had bought utility furniture for the sitting room. The whole house was delightful and it was lovely for my mother. She created a vegetable garden and a lovely flower garden. My father had a job he enjoyed and I was so pleased for them.

After three months on the district we went to Earlham Hall just outside Norwich. It is now part of East Anglia University and is also the birth place of Elizabeth Fry, the Quaker prison reformer. It was a gracious wisteria clad pale red brick building in lovely grounds, which had been sold to the council and was now used as a park. I had spent so many happy times there paddling in the river and catching sticklebacks and minnows. We had picnics in the rose garden watching the white doves swooping down for a drink on the central bird bath. Now I was going to live at Earlham Hall and look after new mothers. I was thrilled. I had never realised how noisy it would be with the raucous cry of the peacocks and the never ending call of the cuckoos. The gamekeeper would be out early shooting rabbits and there was the mournful moo of the cows. Coming back at night from visiting my parents meant a long walk along the tree lined avenue with the owls hooting. I was glad when I reached the front door. At the end of six months I went to London to take my qualifying midwifery examination which I passed. I was now a state certified midwife.

After Norwich, I decided to go to Somerset where I had relatives. That was a salutary experience. The midwifery standards were so poor that the unit was eventually closed.

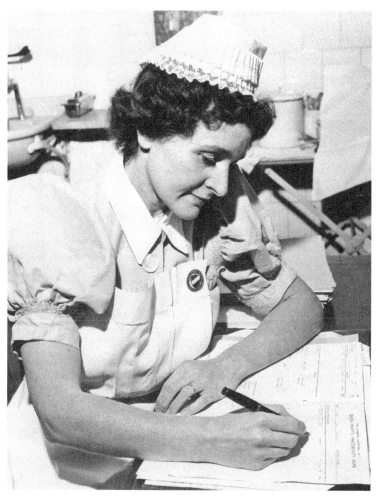

Sister Monteith at her desk in the clinic at Queen Mary's Maternity Home, 1957

However, after being there for three months a letter arrived from the Matron of Queen Mary's inviting me to return as a Staff Midwife, which I gladly accepted.

New life and new babies

When I arrived Easter was approaching. Our sitting room sideboard had racks of eggs. These were all individually decorated with Indian ink by the staff. We had some very artistic midwives and the patients were careful to preserve their eggs as a memento. Christmas was also fun. We always wrote a play and performed it in the large antenatal ward. One year we used the music of the Mikado. I was the mother of triplets and sang:

My name it is Ida

My surname Hope

I've so many children

I scarcely can cope

I'm like the old woman

Who lives in a shoe

And now there is another

And what shall I do?

Rehearsals were hilarious. We had a six foot tall Dutch sister and she and Matron dressed up as premature babies and performed a ballet in slow motion. The laughter and applause continued for about five minutes. All the mothers were there with their husbands. After the comedy we performed a nativity play and I was always Mary. Of course, we had a real Baby Jesus and one year it was a girl, as all the baby boys were crying.

New life and new babies

In 1950, Miss Beaulah had the honour of being accepted as the first Principal of the newly established Midwife Teachers' Training College, for which Aneurin Bevan and Lady Stock, Principal of the London University Westfield College, were the prime movers. The College was situated in an attractive house in beautiful grounds at Kingston upon Thames. (The College is now housed in Surrey University). We were devastated that we were losing our beloved matron but were proud of her well deserved appointment. Miss Benjafield, her deputy, became Matron.

At about this time a friend took me to hear the famous preacher, Leslie Weatherhead. The church was packed and there was standing room only. Leslie Weatherhead was a gifted preacher with a quiet delivery providing helpful and uplifting messages. He also ran the first Christian Psychotherapy Clinic and had written many popular books. About two-hundred people attended the Community Evening on Fridays. It opened at six in the evening and there was a buffet.

Several activities both religious and secular were arranged, ending with an epilogue. The atmosphere was so welcoming and the activities were led by outstanding people. I made many friends. The City Temple, as it was called, played a significant part in my life.

Holidays were not thought of during the war but five years later in 1950 I went to see the Passion Play at Oberammergau, performed every ten years. I was so excited as I had only experienced a day trip to Ostend when I was twelve. My father lent me fifty pounds for the trip. We caught the ferry at Dover for Calais, then the train to Germany. All the trains were very uncomfortable with wooden seats. Cologne was in ruins but we stayed in a newly built hotel and I saw my first large German duvet. Barefoot children were playing along the Rhine riverside as we walked to the station. We cruised past the infamous rocks and then by train to pine tree clad Bavaria. I stayed in the house of a woodcarver in Oberammergau and I still have the delicately carved angels bought from his choir of carvings. We had breakfast on the patio with a dramatic view in the lovely clear mountain air.

The Oberammergau play was in response to a vow made in the seventeenth century by villagers spared by the plagues who vowed to play the life of Christ every ten years. The whole village takes part and it was fascinating to see Mary or Judas as we walked through the village and the men who are all bearded as they were in the time of Jesus. The theatre was like a huge aircraft hangar and the stage was in the open air. The play is in German and we were given an English translation. During the play a storm arose, the thunder reverberated in the mountains and the stage was awash as Judas was about to hang himself.

In the evening we attended a party with people of all nationalities. One group had travelled from Communist controlled East Germany with great risk to themselves.

They had earned money by singing. When they stood in the moonlight singing 'Silent Night' with the cross shining on the top of the mountain we were all visibly moved. I wrote to one of the group in communist East Germany but never heard from them again.

The next day we took the cable car and went to Partenkirchen, now a popular ski resort. This was my first time at the top of a mountain in the snow and looking into Austria I found it so exciting, as I was feeling about the whole wonderful trip!

In 1952 I was accepted for the Midwife Teacher's Diploma Course (now MSc) at Kingston. It was a delightful country house and I was fortunate in living in a cottage in the beautiful grounds with two other students. The course was intense as we were dealing with two lives at every birth. We were to be the tutors of the future. Every week we had to prepare a lecture and deliver it to the class. It was nerve wracking as every aspect was either praised or criticised. It was our posture, expression, delivery as well as the contents and illustrations that were up for comment. The final exams were for anatomy and physiology, and papers written as lectures and this was followed by an oral examination. Only a third of students passed part one as this was called. The second part was also daunting, with a clinical examination of a live patient and a pupil waiting to be taught, and in the presence of a consultant obstetrician with a midwife present. This was followed by being given a subject to prepare in fifteen minutes for a half-hour lecture with a class of students and a consultant obstetrician present. However, I passed. I had not been nervous because I was so looking forward to lunch with the man who would become my husband!

I was then appointed as the Antenatal and Post-natal Clinic Sister and Clinical Tutor, and as we were now administered by the London Hospital I wore their beautiful uniform. It was so well tailored in sky blue cotton with penny sized pearl buttons and large puff sleeves. The pleated lace caps were individually goffered and were very becoming. I so enjoyed my work and never really thought of it as a job. When I was appointed we had no resident doctor so I was responsible for all the antenatal patients. Any mother with an obstetric difficulty was referred to the consultant at his weekly visit. It was a responsibility but we never lost a mother in my twelve years at Queen Mary's. Also we had no case of pre-eclamptic toxaemia in the five years that I was in charge of the clinic. I was forever vigilant having missed a raised blood pressure which nearly resulted in the death of a patient when I was a student midwife. I was summoned to matron and I never forgot that interview. Mothers with tight wedding rings, swollen ankles or raised blood pressure, having the early signs of toxaemia, were put on strict bed rest. If they did not manage this at home they were admitted. I worked closely with Margie Polden, our delightful physiotherapist. Our fathers' classes were such fun and the mothers on their next visit were delighted with the increased care from their husbands.

Meanwhile, in 1952, I fell in love! His name was Lionel Monteith. I met him at the City Temple. He was then a Quantity Surveyor and also a published poet and a member of P.E.N., a prestigious organisation for published writers. After attending the Community Evening on a Friday at the City Temple we would gravitate to a nearby flat where I would hear Lionel reading poetry. At one such meeting he asked me to supper. The next meeting was at the Carol Concert at the Albert Hall. He managed to obtain an arena ticket and during the interval asked me for coffee. I was astonished as Lionel had shaved off his moustache (of which I had expressed a dislike at our previous meeting) and had obtained a ticket for a fully booked concert. Five meetings later, in January, we were engaged, and married on 25th March 1953 by Leslie Weatherhead at The City Temple.

On the news of my impending marriage I was summoned to meet the Matron of the London Hospital. Married staff were not allowed. However, she agreed that I should continue in my present post and work part-time which was forty hours a week including alternate Saturday mornings. I was to be the only married Sister at the London Hospital.

Chapter three
Marriage and parenthood

Let me not to the marriage of true minds
admit impediments

Sonnet 116 by William Shakespeare

It was a warm sunny day when we were married on
'Lady day', 25th March 1953, by Leslie Weatherhead.
I wore an attractive pink woollen dress, pink coat and a
pink hat with a veil. This was an economy wedding as
we could not afford a reception for all our many friends.
My father and mother travelled from Norwich with the
cake. When we arrived at the church Lionel's two half
sisters were already there. Sybil was a Monteith, who
had married an influential and wealthy man and was
used to moving in court circles. She was in black,
in mourning for Queen Mary who had died the day
before. Lionel said that he had turned on the radio and
that it was playing 'The Dead March from Saul'. Eileen
was his second half-sister from his mother's side of the
family and was a nurse.

Our voices echoed in the empty church as we made
our vows, with tears running down my father's face.
We were married for thirty-eight momentous years.

Marriage and parenthood

We all went in Sybil's car to our one roomed flat in Belsize Park. I had made sandwiches the night before and in spite of damp tea towels they were curling at the edges. We partook of Sybil's sherry as we ate cake and after the usual speeches and best wishes we took my parents to the train for Norwich. The next day we began our two week honeymoon at the Manor of God Be-Got which was an old timbered Elizabethan hotel in Winchester High Street.

The large room in Belsize Park had a dining area by a large bay window, a comfortable sitting area in front of a large electric fire, and a wardrobe and bed. The minute kitchen had a 'baby Belling' electric cooker which was either on or off and could not be adjusted. My cooking was a disaster. I also had to cope with a ration book as meat was still rationed.

When I went on duty to Queen Mary's I took the tube every morning from Belsize Park.

Christmas at Belsize Park was very different from Queen Mary's. We had a very warm-hearted minute French landlady. (She gave us a new eiderdown when we left). My parents came to stay in one of her vacant rooms. We cooked Christmas dinner on three floors! The turkey and roast potatoes on one, vegetables, gravy, etc. on another and the pudding on the ground floor. It was quite an adventure. Apart from my parents we had two lonely souls to share it with us but I so missed the camaraderie of Christmas at Queen Mary's.

Marriage and parenthood

Lionel Monteith was a brown eyed, quiet, gentle man, intellectual and an exceptional organiser. He was illegitimate, born to the sister of his father's wife. He was taken from his mother six hours after birth, and fostered until he was a toddler at two and a half. He never saw his beloved foster mother again. He then lived with his birth mother whom he called 'Auntie'. At six years old his half-brother of whom he was fond was killed on a motorbike. His father died from a heart attack when he was nine years old. The early disruptions and emotional damage caused intense depression and anxiety and led him to seek psychotherapy. Leslie Weatherhead recommended a Canadian psychoanalyst and consultant at St Mary's Hospital, Paddington – Dr Percy Bachus. This was to prove a turning point in Lionel's life.

By the next Christmas Lionel was at London University reading theology on a four year course which led to the Diploma in Theology. We moved and had a flat on the other side of the college wall and I was able to walk to Queen Mary's by way of a country lane.

Lionel had to pass an entrance examination that included Greek before he was accepted at New College where he was the senior student in his year, being now aged thirty three. His year known as the troglodytes or cave dwellers were quite hilarious. One day I visited to see the venerable portraits in hall framed in lavatory seats. A student about to become engaged found that his study was bare of furniture with a terrible smell of kipper coming from the radiator.

Marriage and parenthood

We lived on my salary of forty pounds a month until Lionel was granted a two hundred pound annual bursary and an old friend left him one hundred pounds. We delayed having a family until Lionel's fourth year at University. He had decided to become a Congregational Minister training in tandem with the theology course, and through that avenue to start a psychotherapy clinic in the same way as Leslie Weatherhead had done.

The mothers in the antenatal clinic thought I was scared of becoming pregnant whilst I longed for a baby. However, I did become pregnant with twins in 1957, Lionel's fourth year at university. Our friends rallied round with a baby shower – including cots and baby bath and we hardly had to buy anything. We bought a large Harrods twin pram for ten pounds which was fit for royalty. As I was expecting twins I realised I would have double nappies to wash and I had no washing machine. I wrote to the nappy washing service for an interview. I suggested that they provided nappy washing tokens which could be a gift for an expectant mother. They gave me free nappy washing for seven months for which I was so grateful. All did not go well and I went into premature labour at 27 weeks of pregnancy and was admitted to Queen Mary's. My parents were informed and they came immediately to keep house for Lionel. I was only allowed one visitor which was Lionel, of course, and was sedated with chloral for five weeks. At the thirty-second week of pregnancy I developed severe vomiting and was admitted to the London Hospital. I was severely ill and a caesarean was proposed for the next day. Lionel's student year had an all night vigil of prayer for me, and the following day I stopped vomiting and was able to tolerate milk and water. The next day I went into labour and after a four hour first stage I was told that the babies were badly positioned and that I must not push. This was agonising until Mr Brews, Head of the Obstetric Department breezed in and called 'Hold on'. I gratefully inhaled the anaesthetic and a voice in my head kept repeating 'God is suffering, God is suffering'. It was so real and I have never forgotten it.

When I awoke I was the mother of a boy and a girl, Hamish weighed 3lb 11oz and Fiona 3 lb 4 oz. After delivering so many babies I was so disappointed that I had not been conscious at their birth. Sister had put white roses in a vase and Lionel christened our babies. I still have the pressed roses. The babies were in incubators and tube fed with my breast milk. On the fourth day I was awakened by sister and told that Fiona had stopped breathing and now her breathing was erratic. She was prescribed Streptomycin injections and soon recovered. The light shone through her tiny pink starfish hands. My father celebrated the birth of his grandchildren by taking six dozen nappies to the launderette in preparation for their homecoming. He had the attention of all those doing their washing and really enjoyed the experience.

Marriage and parenthood

The babies were born on 3rd October and Lionel was ordained at West Kensington Congregational Church on 7th October. The ordination was taped and so I was able to hear the service. I was discharged from hospital at 12 days and subsequently travelled daily from Hampstead to Whitechapel to give my babies a three minute breast feed. They came home when they weighed four and a half pounds. I breast fed them three hourly and they gained half a pound a week. I fed them simultaneously in bed and propped on cushions and it only took twenty minutes. I fed them for six and a half months. One night I was so tired that we set the alarm for 6am eliminating the nightly feed. We overslept and woke at eight instead of six. All was silent and I thought they were dead. They were fast asleep. The next night they slept until six o'clock to my relief. Life was difficult as we had no fridge, washing machine or running hot water and I was so looking forward to moving. However, I had free nappy washing for seven months!

Our drama and anxiety was not over. Lionel had previously had a chest X-ray because of a persistent cough and was called for a check. When he returned he said that he had a chest abscess and a bed had been booked for him at the Brompton Hospital for the following day. We were just packing his bag when the phone rang to repeat his X-ray. He was clear. The plates had been mixed.

When the babies were six months old I moved into the newly built manse beside the church. We had very little furniture but my wealthy sister-in-law was moving and bequeathed to us beautiful lined curtains, a large Tudor dining table and three beds. We could not afford carpets and Lionel varnished hardboard for the bedroom floors. The ground floors were tiled. It was so wonderful to have a hot bath. We had no fridge or washing machine but we soon acquired those second-hand.

Being a Minister's wife was equivalent to being a marked woman. I felt sympathy for the Queen as I felt my behaviour was being closely monitored, especially when Lionel was wearing his clerical collar. I had all kinds of jobs. The first Christmas I produced a nativity play. I ran a group for our Community Evening; I became Sunday School Superintendent for over one hundred children; supervised tuition for scripture exams; taught the Sunday school teachers;raised money at a jumble sale for a projector and new desks and chairs; made jam and cakes for the bazaars; and so on. I had great empathy with the woman in Joanna Trollopes book 'The Rector's Wife'. And for all our hard work Lionel's stipend was under three hundred pounds per annum. We had wonderful people in the church who would leave various items on the doorstep and mysterious hampers at Christmas. I learnt to cook nourishing meals from lentils, coley, scrag of lamb, mushroom stalks at four pence a quarter of a pound and I had various innovations, which I concocted and stuffed into pancakes. My delicious risotto was enhanced with our homemade potato wine which cost us nine pence a bottle. Clothes and toys were acquired from the jumble sale. As we lived next door we had first choice. One year I bought my winter coat and at the next jumble sale a hat to match. When Lionel became Chaplin at St Mary Abbott's Hospital it eased our finances a little.

When the children were six years old my sister-in-law organised a three feet deep round Harrod's swimming pool to be set up in the garden. This was to be a source of great fun and laughter. At the same time the Austrian niece of a neighbour asked if she could stay with us. Her name was Renate and she was a teacher. She was a great success with the children and subsequently came to us every summer for the next four years.

Lionel's preaching drew people to the services including glamorous Australian ballet dancers from the nearby ballet school. They were far from home and spent Christmas day with us and we were still in contact years later. Any new people who attended the evening service were invited to the manse for tea and scotch pancakes.

I made friends with a former nurse from Great Ormond Street Hospital, Angela Masterton. Her husband John, was a surgeon at U.C.H. and he was so impressed with Lionel that he arranged a meeting for him to meet the U.C.H. Psychotherapy Consultant. Lionel was subsequently sent N.H.S. psychotherapy patients. It was good experience but was not paid.

Rev. Lionel Monteith, Minister of West Kensington Congregational Church, 1953–1970

John invited us to a U.C.H. dance at the Festival Hall. I wore a glamorous off the shoulder red taffeta dress. There was a good band and we danced until dawn. It was so romantic to see the lights on the river and the smell of breakfast cooking. A change from being a minister's wife!

Marriage and parenthood

When the children were three years old my father became seriously ill and was admitted to hospital in Norwich. We were at a Queen Charlotte's dance when my mother rang to say that my father was dying. I took the first train to Norwich but was not in time to see him. I had not known that he was so ill. I brought my mother home with me to live with us. My parents had always spent both Christmas and August with us so it was a second home to my mother. After nine months she left us to stay with her niece who was expecting her fourth child.

The children went to St Mary Abbott's School when they were five years old and settled well and made good progress. However, we moved when they were seven and so they had to leave.

We were sad to leave West Kensington where we had made good friends and met some remarkable people. Our blind and gifted organist would interlace an organ voluntary with a nursery rhyme. He had a great sense of humour. One day I asked him if we could sing the lovely Eleanor Farjeon poem 'Morning has broken' which was in our hymn book. Cat Stevens lived nearby and I often wondered whether he first heard the hymn he made famous at West Kensington Congregational Church.

Before we leave West Kensington I must tell you about dear gentle Anne. She had lived in America where her two children were killed when a fire broke out at a

Roman Catholic convention. She was pregnant with her third child when the priest told her that her children had died because of her own wicked behaviour. Then she had a miscarriage. Her husband threw the bible in the fire and she never entered a church again. Her next pregnancy was an ectopic one in her fallopian tube. She nearly died and the tubal pregnancy meant that she could have no more children. Eventually they returned to England and lived next door to one of our church members. Lionel visited her and eventually persuaded her to come to a service. She was scared as she thought that because of past events there would be divine retribution. However, she became more and more confident and when she joined the church as a member at a communion service tears of joy streamed down her face. She was such a lovely person. She always knew everybody's name in the shops, the post office and the church. She was the 'sewing lady' at the Brompton Hospital and she made crocheted mats and dollies to sell at the bazaar. One day she came to me seeing I was stressed and said 'How can I help you, dear?'. She visited me every two weeks and I remember her quiet counsel 'Always tackle the worst job first dear'. Realising our straitened circumstances Anne saved her pension and bought us a chicken every two weeks as we could not afford a Sunday joint. She loved the children and made little trousers for Hamish. She befriended our blind organist and eventually came to church with a small group of blind people. She developed cancer and was unable to have an operation because of a heart condition.

Marriage and parenthood

My husband knew of two others who needed help, one with glaucoma and the other with a leg ulcer. Unbeknown to the Church my husband held a weekly healing service. The ulcer healed, the glaucoma lessened and Anne's cancer vanished. She lived until she was over ninety. She could have been embittered by her tragic life. Instead she was loving, understanding and full of compassion for others.

Chapter four
Aylesbury Estate, London SE1

I have seen some flowers come in stony places
An Epilogue by John Masefield

We moved to Lambeth to live in a five storey Regency
House in Kennington Road. This was to be our manse.
The Church was Christ Church and Upton Chapel,
an amalgamation of two churches – Congregational
and Baptist. It was near Westminster and opposite
Lambeth North Station in an ideal situation for a
Psychotherapy clinic. I was reminded of a Robert Frost
poem 'The Road Not Taken':

> *Two roads diverged in a wood, and I*
> *I took the one less travelled by,*
> *And that has made all the difference.*

The right choice is so important in life.

The manse was fully decorated for us, but without
central heating, so that we tended to live in the
smallest room in the basement. My husband's book
lined study on the first floor had an electric fire and
was a magnificent room. We put an oil heater in
the hall, hoping that the heat would rise to take the
chill off other rooms. Lionel began to build up his

psychotherapy practice seeing patients in the manse, his training having been supervised by Dr Bachus.

The children attended a school at the Oval. It was a very different catchment area from the Kensington school. Hamish was bullied. Children always know if there is some difference in a child. Hamish was unable to make friends and his behaviour was sometimes inexplicable.

It was not until 1991 that we knew that Hamish had Asperger's Syndrome. Fiona protected him as much as possible. We had a teacher friend who told us of the small classes in Westminster. The children were transferred to Burdett Coutts, a Church of England Primary school where they were very happy.

I started training as a family planning nurse and enjoyed my walk to the clinic through East Street market in Walworth, with the joking and salacious asides from the stall holders. The clinic was one of the first founded by Marie Stopes, the family planning pioneer. Family planning was still only officially for married women, and the 'others' were seen in the back room. The clinic work was sessional and I was always home for the children who came home by bus.

At this time our finances had improved with my earnings, and my husband with his psychotherapy practice felt that I too should enter the mysterious world of psychotherapy. I needed to understand Lionel's profession and I felt that somehow I was responsible for Hamish's condition. Mothers so often feel guilty if there is some physical or behavioural problem with their children. Lionel said that the 'inner world' is so important that I should have psychoanalysis by a therapist trained at the Institute of Psychoanalysis, whose training required analysis five times a week. When I started my therapy I lay on a couch like a fish on a slab in a large high-ceilinged room, and the analyst was unseen. He rarely said anything and at first I was struck dumb. I have always been so grateful for the therapeutic experience. I learned so much about myself, and became more understanding of other people and I know it helped my family.

My husband meanwhile realised that although the church was newly built it also possessed an historic tower, partly built with American money. The foundation stone had been laid by Abraham Lincoln's son, to commemorate the end of slavery, and the tower was called 'The Lincoln Tower'. When we took the large key and opened the heavy door, we were met by cobwebs and dust. The rooms were full of old pews and broken furniture. When the spacious rooms were cleared we realised that it would make an ideal clinic. It was like the tardis. The winding stairs led up to three large rooms, the room downstairs could be used as an office or waiting room, and there was space for a toilet to be built.

Aylesbury Estate, London SE1

Renate, our young Austrian friend had introduced us to the Anglo-Austrian Society. They arranged au pairs and exchange visits. As our new home was so large, and Lionel was treating patients at home and I was working, we decided that we could afford an au pair. So Austrian Ingrid arrived. She fitted in well. She had trained as a teacher and was good with the children. Au pairs, we found, usually had problems, and Ingrid's mother was schizophrenic.

She sent Ingrid endless vitamin tablets and batteries. In fact when Ingrid left she filled her thigh length boots with all her mother's gifts. Her mother threatened to come for Christmas and sleep on the floor. We contacted the Austrian Embassy for a restraining order to prevent Ingrid's mother from entering the country. Ingrid and I completely redecorated the Lincoln Tower. I perched nervously on an extremely long ladder as I painted the high ceilings. Then there were the extensive walls, and, lastly, the winding stone stairs and banisters. I was very proud of my French polished banisters. Ingrid was an amazing worker. We used our limited funds to carpet the rooms with red hair cord carpet. A doctor friend informed us that a certain nursing organisation was moving to Geneva, and that they were selling their furniture. We bought beautiful desks and filing cabinets, and also some very solid chairs. We painted the filing cabinets white and in 1966 the first consulting room was ready, with a psychotherapy couch and my husband's name on the door.

Ingrid stayed with us for a year and became part of the family. She enjoyed our home experience, being moved continually from flat to flat in Austria, after her mother was divorced. She went to Morley College to improve her English and she was a willing helper in the home. She left us to take a teaching job in Germany. A few months later she was accepted as a student at Hamburg University to read prehistory. She worked with Leakey, the famous anthropologist, in Africa and then came to Cambridge University for a year. On graduating she became the custodian of Hamburg antiquities. We eventually lost touch when she married a student she had met at University.

Lionel hoped that his practice would grow. It was not done to advertise and patients only came by personal recommendation. It was difficult when patients recovered and were not replaced!

However, Lionel negotiated with the church for a colleague to share the services and half of the stipend. He eventually relinquished his role as a Congregational Minister to work full time as a psychotherapist.

The clinic was registered as the 'Lincoln Memorial Clinic for Psychotherapy' and became a limited company and eventually a charity, and I became a Director and Trustee, and other Trustees were also appointed.

My husband was soon joined in the Tower by Tom Forsyth, another psychotherapist. Tom was instrumental in introducing Lionel to other psychoanalysts who became a significant part of the Lincoln organisation, with Gil Parker becoming the first Dean of Studies. She gradually set up a psychotherapy training course. Lionel was determined to have a training course equal to that of the Tavistock Clinic, with only qualified psychoanalysts as tutors. At the present time the Lincoln Roster shows nearly one hundred and thirty therapists, is a well respected training organisation and has now joined with two other psychotherapy organisations – the L.C.P. (The London Centre for Psychotherapy) and the B.A.P. (The British Association of Psychotherapy) to become the British Psychotherapy Foundation. Being a much larger organisation will hopefully mean negotiations with the Minister of Health to include psychotherapy within the N.H.S.

At about that time John Kelnar, who had been Tom's analyst and was a consultant at the Tavistock Clinic, needed a venue for a course for marriage guidance counsellors. Lionel offered him the ground floor room in the Tower. From this beginning the Lincoln counselling courses evolved. I was involved in the publicity for the courses and we had two thousand applications a year. The course was for a hundred students. The first two terms were for lectures. In the third term the student was required to present a case study in a group of ten, led by a psychotherapist. At the last session, certificates were awarded stating course attendance.

The greatest number of students were psychiatric nurses, social workers, teachers, police and those in need of counselling knowledge. There were eventually two courses a year, with one hundred students in each, at St Thomas's Hospital and the Middlesex Hospital. The income from these courses enabled Lionel at a later stage to buy premises to house the Lincoln offices and a consulting room.

Meanwhile, the Church owned a couple of retirement homes in Ashford, Middlesex. My mother was fortunate in being offered a charming flat. There was a resident warden, a lovely garden, the mobile library visited every week and shops were nearby. It was good for my mother to have her own home and to be independent again.

We had a housing problem when Lionel left the church. We needed to buy our own house. We found a four bedroomed house in Camberwell and lived there until 1994. We borrowed money from my mother for the deposit. We were still only just managing as the setting up of the clinic had depleted our resources. This was the first house Lionel had owned and he was in his fortieth year.

The children were so pleased that our swimming pool had been moved from our pocket sized garden in Lambeth to our new garden. It was such fun especially when Daddy was tipped off the lilo. We had a full-sized table tennis table on the veranda where Lionel and

Hamish became expert players. We had barbecues whenever possible and the garden was a haven for our busy lives.

Hamish and Fiona travelled by train from Denmark Hill to Victoria to their new secondary schools in Westminster, which were Grey Coat Hospital and Westminster City. When Hamish was interviewed for a place at the school, we were also present. He was asked by the Headmaster if he had any questions about the school. Hamish embarrassingly asked the Headmaster his age. We squirmed in our seats. Hamish was at first refused a place but Lionel appealed against this decision as Hamish had been one of the top three boys at primary school. Hamish was lost without Fiona, and although he excelled academically at first, coping with the other boys and adolescence, became insurmountable hurdles. He would come home with his blazer dusty, and be quiet and dispirited. He was unable to tell us of his problems, because he did not know what they were. The yearly meeting with the form tutor shed no light on Hamish's behaviour. I do wish we had known of his autism then.

When the children were twelve they each had bikes, and Hamish a two-stroke motor bike at seventeen. Before going on the road they went to the cycling proficiency course at Crystal Palace.

There were school holidays in Wales for Hamish and a Mediterranean cruise for Fiona. At thirteen they had their first Anglo-Austrian exchange holiday which was meticulously arranged and a great success. Fiona is still in touch with Lies, her Austrian exchange friend, forty years later. Hamish coped and seemed to enjoy his two stays in Austria.

Fiona was busy in her teenage years with the Duke of Edinburgh Award Scheme. It certainly developed Fiona's independence and experience of life. For the gold award there were considerable challenges. She organised a hundred mile bike ride with two friends. They had to map out a route with reasons for their choice. They also had to give brief histories of the places they visited. Fiona was a weekly volunteer on the obstetric ward at the Middlesex Hospital. She cruised on the Thames with the river police. She made three spectacular stuffed characters from the television programme 'The Magic Roundabout'. They were the large-headed and blank-eyed Florence, Brian the snail and the cuddly dog Dougal, covered in rug wool. When Fiona went to Buckingham Palace to receive her award she was told that if she smiled the Duke of Edinburgh would speak to her and he duly did. He asked her if she intended to do medicine and she replied in the negative. Instead she left school at eighteen to read geophysical sciences at Southampton University. Hamish managed three O-levels and was accepted as a clerk at the Southwark Inland Revenue Office living in a civil service hostel and attending psychotherapy three times a week in Harley Street. The therapist was experienced in treating young people. It was expensive but we so wanted to help Hamish. It was especially distressing for Lionel. He said I can help my patients but not my own son.

I was very concerned about the traffic on our road. There had been several bad accidents and one death. This was the road the children had to cross. I organised a petition and collected five hundred names for a safe crossing or bollards. Neighbours helped in monitoring the number of cars passing through the day and we made graphs of the traffic. I contacted the police and the head of the nearby primary school. Ten of us were invited to a meeting at Southwark Town hall where we presented our petition. Eventually bollards were installed followed by traffic lights.

I was approached by a pharmaceutical firm to be a family planning consultant and to lecture nurses in hospitals in south-east London. I went to inner London teaching hospitals and as far east as Bow, which I did for two years as well as being a clinic nurse. One day a patient at the family planning clinic told me of her health visitor training and that it was salaried. I was very interested in the course, as it fitted in with my family commitments. I soon applied for the Health Visitor's training course and was accepted.

While I was at the South Bank Polytechnic on the health visitors' diploma course Radio London rang to ask if they could interview a mature student. I was chosen, being the oldest student. I enjoyed the interview and was asked if I would take part in a family planning phone in programme. This was an intimidating experience. A question master, with four of us sat around a table, each with a microphone, being asked questions by the general public for two hours. The other three people were experts in their field. They were the Head of the Family Planning Organisation, a geneticist and a family planning doctor. My husband rang with a question. 'A Camberwell clergyman has rung in with this question' the question master said and I knew it was Lionel. 'And now Mary Monteith will you answer this'. My heart would pound at the questions directed to me. Lionel taped it all and the family were glued to the radio.

Radio London held a Saturday morning children's programme and my children went. They met Rolf Harris and other celebrities. Fiona read one of her poems on radio and won a prize, which to her disgust was a gardening book.

On passing the Diploma in Health Visiting I was assigned to the new Health Centre on the Aylesbury Estate. The Walworth East Street market was nearby, and also near my former family planning clinic so that I knew the area very well. The stallholders always seemed to be cheery and joked amongst themselves. John who ran the salad stall was tall and handsome and he would say to the old ladies 'You look lovely today darling' and they loved it.

Aylesbury Estate, London SE1

There were two other health visitors at the Centre, both Irish, one from the Republic who was very quiet, and the other Ann from Northern Ireland, who became my friend. We were each allocated to about one hundred families. One of my areas was a road of old houses due for demolition and the residents did not want to move. They all knew one another and kept their doors open for the neighbours' children. The difference from the friendly street to the Aylesbury Estate was tangible. People had been housed indiscriminately and the construction of the houses did not promote neighbourliness. Each front door had a porch which screened next door's front door. No time for a chat when collecting the milk bottles. These porches provided places for truant schoolchildren to hide. The truancy rate in Southwark was 20 per cent in the 1970s. One morning I received a shocking phone call from the Medical Officer of Health saying that two children had been scalded to death with pure steam coming out of the tap when they tried to wash their doll. They were three and four years old. In the 1970s the Aylesbury Estate was shown on a documentary on television stating that it was so badly planned that it should be demolished. However, the Council continued building it and waited until 2012 before alterations were made at last. Problem families were often clumped together. I remember one Irish family with eight children and no furniture except beds. I procured some necessary wardrobes for them and came to know the mother very well.

She was a good mother and loved her children. There was always a huge pot on the cooker. It was porridge for breakfast and a nourishing stew for dinner. The washing was done daily by the eldest children at the communal launderette. No ironing was done but every morning clean clothes were extracted from the black plastic bag of clean laundry, the older ones dressing the younger ones. There were no chairs or table and the children sat on the floor to eat their porridge. Mrs Connolly's eighth child had Down's syndrome which was very sad and distressed Mrs Connolly. We were concerned that she might become pregnant again. She was badly in need of the repair of the overstretched muscle supporting the uterus. She was persuaded to have the operation and with her permission a hysterectomy was performed to our relief. I met Mrs Connolly in the market years later, and she was smartly dressed and told me of the success of her children.

Door-to-door salesmen on the Aylesbury Estate, would persuade mothers to buy items which they could ill afford. Bills were not paid and the gas would be cut off.

Mothers did not have the cooking skills to save money. They would buy a chicken pie instead of a chicken which would have lasted much longer. Children would have a 'chip butty' for dinner, whilst father had a steak.

Mothering and parenting skills consisted so often of a smack or a threat of 'I'll kill you'.

West Indian mothers were often not aware of the importance of early nurturing. The baby would be placed in a day nursery at six weeks old and the mother would work in order to buy the baby Marks & Spencer clothes. Children who had been looked after by their grandmothers in the Caribbean, were sent for to find that there were siblings in England whom they had never met.

This caused endless problems. It was a relief to talk to Ann about our mutual difficulties or else Miss Foster, our wise health visitor supervisor.

Our weekly mothers' group was very important as we tried to help with parenting skills. They were not keen on immunisation and on one occasion I asked them to bring their baby photographs and pinned them on a board and had an identity competition. It was great fun. Then I produced two large oil paintings of my great grandmothers. I asked them what diseases had been prevalent when they were alive. They were shocked with the cholera statistics and that of other infectious diseases. They started to see the reason for immunisation and the uptake increased. I always remember a Christmas meeting. My health visitor colleague was very musical and had a melodious singing voice. She brought her guitar and sang carols while the mothers made Christmas decorations for the elderly women who attended chiropody. I had sprayed yoghurt pots and twigs with a silver spray, and invited the mothers to bring milk bottle tops and they made very attractive table decorations.

The chiropodists were really touched. The group became such a success that they founded a second group at the community centre and even went to France for the day. Later, at another clinic we organised a Christmas party. We laid a paper table cloth on the floor and sat the tiny children alongside and fed them with jelly and crisps. We gave the mothers sherry and homemade mince pies. Father Christmas came with a huge sack containing balloons for each child. A party on a shoestring and how everybody enjoyed it.

The Irish headmaster of Paragon Boys' School on the Old Kent Road rang our supervisor to ask for a lecturer in sex education for one hundred and fifty teenaged boys. Of course I was the chosen one and my heart sank. I organised a parents' evening, and a doctor and my husband in his clerical collar came to support me. It was important that I had the permission of the parents before I started the six week course. I outlined my plan and information and all was well. I arranged to see the boys in groups of ten twice weekly. On my first day ten boys slouched into the room chewing gum which I asked them to deposit in the waste-paper basket. Other boys had their faces pressed against the glass door which was locked. Later the glass was covered. My first session was on growth and nutrition, and the first thing we discussed was breakfast which the majority had not had. The next week they were more alert having had some form of nourishment. Several of them, although thirteen years of age could not read, so I had to use visual aids and diagrams.

One day I went to collect my keys from an adjoining classroom which was in uproar although there was a teacher in attendance. If my class became inattentive I always threatened to leave, which had the right effect. My most effective class was when the day's headline in the *Sun* newspaper read 'Sixteen year old boy father of triplets'. The boys were shocked into attention and an excellent discussion ensued. I was the school 'Sex lady' and the boys would meet my car and carry my equipment to the classroom. At the last session with the one hundred and fifty boys, I showed a film of the development of the foetus which had amazing photography.

I heaved a sigh of relief when after a year, this assignment was completed.

Lionel meanwhile was seeing patients in the Tower and gradually establishing the Lincoln Centre. The first Chairman of Trustees was Eric Edwards, who was also Chair of the Portman Clinic, an organisation to help ex-prisoners. After Eric died there was a succession of psychoanalysts as chairman, followed by Anton Obholzer, who was also Chairman of the Tavistock Clinic, and was a great support to the Lincoln for many years.

We held Clinic parties in the Tower. It was an amazing experience being in the presence of so many therapists, each of them assessing the other. How am I today? At the first party we cooked a twenty pound turkey, and insulating it with newspaper it kept hot, and Lionel carved it to great acclaim. I had cooked all the food for the party, and one of the wives suggested that they should provide the desserts in future and I thankfully agreed.

Chapter five

Newpin and new hope

Such love I cannot analyse
Friendship by Elisabeth Jennings

My experiences on the Aylesbury Estate made me long to be able to have the power to change and improve the life of the families.

In 1975, with the children leaving home, and the Guy's District Health Education Officer's post becoming vacant I decided to study for the C.N.A.A. Diploma in Health Education, at the South Bank Polytechnic. The course widened my knowledge of the considerable challenges ahead. One of the projects linking me again with the Aylesbury Estate was researching hearing in three year old children. I acquired twenty nursery rhyme booklets and a tape recorder. I was sad to note the many children who did not know a nursery rhyme and the parents who never read to their children. I found two children who were profoundly deaf and had never been assessed at the clinic. The good news was that they were referred to Guy's early enough to develop speech and attend a normal school.

When I received my diploma, I sat with the gowned degree students and was called to the rostrum to receive my certificate. I was thrilled.

In 1976 I was interviewed for the Health Education Officer post and was successful. I was the first trained health education officer to be appointed to Guy's Health District, which covered most of Southwark. Previously, the department had focused on safety in the home and first aid, providing posters and visual aids. I had a very different agenda. Statistics showed that heart disease was the greatest cause of death and prevention of this was to be central to my policy, focussing on a healthy diet, exercise and no smoking. Secondly, I would need to educate the educators, the first of whom proved to be the home helps! They were a lovely group of women and they were receptive and amazed at being 'Home Educators'.

My first office was a converted shop with a huge plate glass window, at the Elephant and Castle. It is now a fast food cafe! I only had a staff of three. They were a man who was good at creating visual aids and being a projectionist, a secretary with constant migraine and a driver of our small van used for delivering films.

Security of the shop was a problem, with thieves entering the roof at night and stealing valuable equipment. My typewriter and new brief case were stolen from my office, and muggings in the pedestrian subways were common. At Christmas, with only one member of staff in the basement, three youths entered, and became offensive and threatening. I called out and was relieved to hear footsteps. The young thugs soon disappeared. When my husband heard of the incident he contacted Dr. James, the medical officer to whom I was accountable. I was moved into Castle House, the main building housing the community health and social service managers. I now had a private office, a large lecture hall and a workshop.

Now I was among the managers I decided to announce my presence by inviting them to a Health Education lunch for one pound each. We cleared the workshop, transforming it into a buffet with homemade lentil soup (with recipe) and wholemeal rolls and an apple. The community dietician provided the cakes, as well as a ten minute talk. In the next room we showed our very amusing Walt Disney heart disease film, and fitted all this into one hour. We had two sittings and I would meet people afterwards, who would tell me that they had made my lentil soup!

Within the year I was at Mary Sheridan House opposite Guy's main gates. It was a lovely house and I was on the ground floor. My office was a large room which I made into a comprehensive leaflet library, and screened off my filing cabinets and desk to make my office. The advantage of this was that I was able to contact many key people. They would sign the visitor's book with their name, occupation and reason for their visit which was very helpful to me. I felt like a spider weaving my web. By now I had two full time health education officers with degrees, an artist with a community arts degree and a new secretary. My annual department allowance was £6000 so it was vital that I educate the educators, remembering that my main aim was to prevent heart disease with emphasis on stopping smoking, diet and exercise. Health visitors played a significant role in educating the community. They ran weekly mothers groups and I provided them with a list of subjects for the mothers to choose for themselves. The hospital dietitian was enthusiastic in helping me and the community. The most popular subject was marriage guidance (Relate). Eventually a marriage guidance counsellor was available on a regular basis at the Aylesbury Health Centre. The new concept of baby massage was introduced to the health visitors by the author of a book on the subject, who stressed the importance of massage, forming a bond between mother and baby and inducing sleep. It was a useful tool, especially for some of our mothers.

The health centre staff were people of various disciplines. There were health visitors, midwives, chiropodists, district nurses and speech therapists. I introduced lunch time yoga classes at three main health centres. Staff of the different disciplines who normally did not speak to one another now became friendly, interchanging ideas. I never expected this positive outcome.

I held regular six monthly seminars for the health visitors. Pharmaceutical firms, of which I approved, provided excellent lunches and would show a film. The day's seminar would begin at 10am with two lectures before lunch. After lunch in the afternoon there would be time for discussion.

Other community nurses such as district nurses and midwives, could only manage a half-day seminar which would be carefully negotiated to suit their day.

When I was a health visitor I had noticed that the clinic nurses were under used and bored. Every month we gave the clinics an educational theme with posters and leaflets. I decided to invite the clinic nurses to six monthly seminars to expand their knowledge on the subjects chosen. They were each given a research form to be used in the clinic when they questioned the mothers. The information was collated at the end of the year in a final seminar. The nurses really enjoyed the research, giving them extra status.

A new book was published on breastfeeding written by two doctors, and I invited the doctors to chair a breastfeeding conference, inviting heath visitors and midwives. The lecture theatre on the 23rd floor of Guy's Tower was booked. My problem was lunch! There was a wonderful shop in the Borough High Street which sold six inch wide baps with lavish fillings. I ordered about one hundred, and cut them in half and bought pounds of apples at the market. This was lunch for which I charged a pound, Guy's providing tea and coffee. I was so annoyed at the way baby food firms gave samples of baby milk to health visitors at their conferences, and 'bounty bags' were issued free with samples of baby milk, when mothers were discharged, to encourage bottle feeding. There was quite a scandal when a baby food firm advertised widely in Africa, persuading mothers to bottle feed, and the consequence was baby deaths from gastro-enteritis.

Schools were looked after by one of my health education officers who had also been a teacher. She visited schools giving talks and seminars for the teachers. I visited nursery schools and found that the children's drinks and sweets were laced with an excess of sugar, and the white bread sandwiches had the crusts removed!

We visited senior citizen groups, giving talks and showing films. We introduced soft ball games to stimulate circulation, which were really enjoyed.

The next target group was the hospital where there were sister tutors, nurses, medical students and the catering staff. The sister tutors were very helpful and sent the student nurses to us to collect information for their health education projects. We had a small library, filing cabinets with information and desks at which they could work. The medical students were sent to talk to mothers' groups and to teenagers in a comprehensive school. The aim was to encourage understandable communication between medical students and various groups. Feedback from the medical students and lectures were dealt with by my other education officer. I arranged two exhibitions for the special needs of the catering staff at Guy's and New Cross Hospitals. The kitchen staff, especially, needed advice about shoes and feet, and also posture, so apart from the usual health information there was a chiropodist and a physiotherapist with a long mirror to demonstrate posture.

We held two exhibitions in Guy's colonnade which was rather windy on both occasions. It was an excellent venue, as the Guy's staff passed by and were intrigued by the stalls and information.

Health education exhibition: The dental table with dentist, Polly Munday

Our first exhibition in industry was at Sainsbury's head office, in their attractive dining area and was supported by Lord Sainsbury. How we loved the delicious food as we were offered lunch. Professor Spector came and monitored blood pressures only to discover that the head of their medical department had severe hypertension and was sent home immediately. Blood pressure monitoring and screening were subsequently part of the policy of their medical department. We visited Sainsbury's several times and it was always a great success. They subsequently built a gym, which was very well used.

Nine hundred employees of the Post Office Telecommunications headquarters for the south central area attended our next exhibition. The lung capacity machine brought by staff from the Department of Respiratory Medicine persuaded fifty employees to stop smoking and the buffet food was changed to healthier options.

Then we visited the Gas Board at their outlet on the Old Kent Road where they made a video of our exhibition which was sent to other Gas Board outlets. We subsequently had demand from other parts of the country which of course we could not meet.

An exhibition at Associated Biscuits was difficult because of their mainly immigrant staff. Hellmann's pickle factory on the Old Kent Road was an amazing experience with West Indian women in charge of huge vats of pickle, pervading the whole atmosphere with the strong oniony smell. I was intrigued that their eyes were unaffected by the onions. The answer was that one gets used to it!

One day, a tutor from Southwark College visited my leaflet library and the consequence was an exhibition for her needy teenagers. It was a difficult exhibition as for some, healthy living was not on their agenda. However, the sex education information was well attended.

We would not have been able to do these exhibitions without the help of the enthusiastic and experienced professional help, especially of the community dietician. They really enjoyed it as they were able to make a real impact on those who would not normally have access to such expert information.

I was involved in so many areas, one of which was a real challenge. I was asked by a Town Hall official if I would talk to a group of redundant dustmen. I started my talk by telling them that they were the statisticians of the Borough. They knew those who drank and ate too much and I immediately had their attention. After the amusing Walt Disney film on the prevention of heart disease, I then had them all relaxing with closed eyes. I pointed out how their active life had been beneficial in preventing heart disease, but the drivers now needed to concentrate on exercise.

My days were very busy starting at eight thirty in the
morning, but I loved my job. Guy's Hospital staff were
so friendly and welcoming, and Dr James to whom I
made my monthly report gave me freedom and more
or less autonomy. I kept up with the latest statistics and
health issues visiting a friend who was a Director at
the King's Fund where there was a wealth of important
information. I also visited the National Children's Bureau
and the Health Education Council who published
useful leaflets. I bought relevant books for our library
and a significant one for me was by Wendy Cooper
which was about the menopause. I was faced with
the enormous task of providing health education in
Southwark and I was menopausal. My energy levels
were down and I had other debilitating symptoms.
At the back of Wendy Coopers' book was a list of
clinics. My doctor, when asked for a letter of referral
declined and said I would get cancer. However, my
friendly family planning doctor provided the necessary
letter. I was so fortunate as the consultant was John
Studd, who has never wavered in his support of H.R.T.
and is now a Professor and on the Advisory Board of
the British Menopause Society. Hormonal treatment
for the menopause was still a new treatment. I had
blood tests, three monthly vaginal examinations and
a yearly endometrial biopsy. My pills were supplied by
the hospital dispensary. Within days I began to feel
better and my energy returned. My arthritic hands
became pain free as did all the other symptoms. I
am ninety and still on H.R.T. The latest information
states that H.R.T. increases a slight risk of breast

cancer but it offers protection against cardiovascular disease, osteoporosis, colon cancer and dementia, and enhances the quality of life. Dr Heather Currie, is an editor of the British Menopause Society and gave this information in her June, 2012 journal *Menopause Matters*. I do not think I would be typing this if I were not on H.R.T. I walk every day and am not on any other medication. As there are now more people over fifty in our population it is important that our doctors understand the benefits of H.R.T. Both Menopause International and the British Menopause Society have the latest research and provide excellent conferences.

Recently on the front page of the *Daily Telegraph* there was news of a new H.R.T. called Duavee which has been developed in the U.S.A. It is oestrogen only with no progestogen and contains Bazedoxifene which blocks breast cancer cells. It has been tested in the U.S.A. in a study of six thousand women and found that it not only prevented breast cancer but also prevented osteoporosis and menopausal symptoms and had no side effects. It is an exciting breakthrough for people who have had breast cancer and can now safely use H.R.T. I hope this will soon be available in the U.K.

At this time too my mother died. She had been making a cup of tea when she had a stroke. Her plight convinced me of the wisdom of taking H.R.T. She had lost six inches in height and suffered rib fractures. She also had severe arthritis and hip replacements were not then available. H.R.T. seemed to have stopped my emerging arthritis which had already started in my hands. My mother was so brave and battled on with all her disabilities. She was always my great friend.

As for my family there were changes. Fiona was enjoying university and had met another student who was to become my lovely son-in-law. Hamish had been unable to continue his job at the Inland Revenue office and after two years was told to leave. Three times a week psychotherapy for two years was not the answer and our doctor sent him to the Maudsley Hospital, suspecting schizophrenia. He was given a range of treatments which rendered him very thirsty and restless. After experiencing various living conditions it was obvious that he could not live on his own, and needed substantial support. It is so good now that early diagnosis of Asperger's syndrome can lead to useful and fulfilling lives.

My husband was very busy working long hours. He saw his first patient at eight-twenty in the morning and was dealing with referrals and the administration of the Lincoln Clinic until nine o'clock at night. We would then relax, play scrabble and have a glass of wine.

However, the condition and treatment of Hamish was always on our minds.

My job at Guy's was not only an escape from home problems, but a chance to initiate activities and give information which would help people. Dr James called me to his office one day to discuss the possibility of teenage counselling to prevent crime and teenage pregnancies. Also, our school truancy rate was one of the highest in the country being about twenty per cent. I had already met two people working for a charity counselling young teenagers. We decided to have a meeting of representatives from I.L.E.A., Social Services, the Health Service plus two charity workers. The outcome was that each of the services gave ten thousand pounds, which was enough to finance a property and provide counsellors opposite a large comprehensive school off the Old Kent Road. This became known as T.I.N. (Teenage Information Network), and I am sure saved many catastrophes.

However, one thing constantly on my mind was the plight of the young mothers on the Aylesbury Estate.

I had been asked by Dr James to increase the number of women attending parent craft. I knew that this request was not an option as women on the estates did not like health visitors or social workers, thinking of them as 'do gooders'. We knew of the depression and deprivation and we felt that a twenty-four hour emergency telephone line might be the answer, but it was thought to be too expensive to install. Helping agencies such as The Marriage Guidance Council and the National Childbirth Trust were based in middle-class areas, and were outside the district.

Newpin and new hope

Thinking of the success of the Teenage Information Network meeting I called a meeting of those who were working with the women on the estates. There were voluntary groups, a community midwife, a senior nursing officer for health visitors and myself. We had several meetings with various personnel and eventually decided on a name and a format. Mothers would be trained and become befrienders. The organisation would be called Newpin, standing for New Parent Infant Network. The name coined by Diana Cawston, the senior nursing officer. Meanwhile, I had met Willem Van Dem Eyken who was writing a book about a similar organisation called 'Homestart' which trained mothers in parent craft to go into homes to help families. Newpin was to grow into something a little different.

We decided that if we were to raise money we would have to form a charity. I contacted the Guy's solicitor, Peter Clarke, and he was a great support with all the legal issues. Secondly, we decided that we should have a research team from the beginning to convince funders that Newpin was worth funding. We were very fortunate in having the help and interest of three professionals: Andrea Pound, a psychologist, based at the Tavistock Clinic; Maggie Mills, a lecturer in the department of psychology at Bedford College; and a consultant psychiatrist from the Maudsley Hospital. They eventually produced a summary of all their work. Andrea Pound wrote a book succinctly describing the work of Newpin.

Newpin and new hope

In January 1980 the trustees were elected so that the trust deed could be submitted to the Charity Commissioners, and we became a charity in July 1980. The original trustees were:

- Pauline Armstrong, National Childbirth Trust Co-ordinator for Lewisham
- Joan Kedge, Divisional Nursing Officer, Community Nursing
- Dr Margaret Lynch, Community Paediatrician
- Mary Monteith, District Health Education Officer
- Phyllis Smith, Child Abuse Co-ordinator, Southwark Social Services
- Mary Thompson, Divisional Nursing Officer, Midwifery and Paediatrics, Guy's
- Katherine Tyler, Community Health Council.

Now that we were a charity we could appeal for money. I approached National Westminster Bank who generously lent me a retiring member of staff for a year. I gave her a desk and a telephone, and she helped with the appeal letters. I hated begging for money which required my visiting various charities. Eventually we raised over £11,000 with a promise of £5000 a year for the next three years, and we could then think of a venue and the appointment of a co-ordinator.

One day I was visiting an infant welfare clinic which was on the ground floor of a large house which had belonged to the mistress of the Duke of Marlborough. It was a solid building with three floors, and I discovered that the first and second floors were vacant. This was Sutherland House in Sutherland Square in Walworth. I enquired whether it could be used for Newpin. It was ideal, our solicitor obtained a twenty-five year lease and Guy's provided the furnishings.

The next step was the co-ordinator. We appointed Anne Jenkins, who was to prove an excellent choice. I had known Anne for several years. She was a health visitor, working for a doctor in Walworth and was highly commended. She was a mother of four teenage children and was also a midwife. She ticked all the right boxes.

The media initially gave Newpin considerable publicity: in the *Evening Standard*, on the radio, on 'Womans' Hour' and in films on the B.B.C. and I.T.V.

Newpin opened in 1982, those present being Margaret Harrison, founder of 'Homestart', Esther Rantzen and the Mayor of Southwark. Esther was so good with the mothers. She had brought her son Joshua, whom she was breastfeeding at the time and the women were fascinated. We felt it important that these women should receive expert help with a trained group therapist and weekly sessions became part of their course. As Anne Jenkins wrote in the annual report in 2000 'We help to break the cyclical effect of destructive family behaviour and empower women to gain control of their lives'. The aims are as follows:

- Assist in the prevention of all forms of child abuse.
- Support parents and children using our centres by raising self-esteem, confidence and self-determination.
- Work to improve the mental health of users who may be experiencing depression and loss of identity.

Providing structured opportunities that enable children and parents to develop more positive relationships, first within and then beyond Newpin.

Newpin always had a welcoming homely atmosphere. There was a drop-in centre, kitchen, washing machine, playgroup with educational toys and always the chance to talk with a befriender who would listen. Some of these mothers had never experienced love, or a friend. Some had been abused and brought up in care. At Newpin they would start to reach their life potential. Some of them trained on to become Newpin co-ordinators. There were parent craft classes, and courses for all needs including fathers' classes. A mother summed it all up saying 'I would like to pack up Newpin in a suitcase and take it around to everyone and say "Have a slice of that. It will do you good"'.

In the year 2000 there were twenty Newpins and the numbers of people helped were 339 families, 565 children (105 of those on the child protection register) and 157 women in therapeutic support groups. Now there is only one Newpin, and that is in Southwark in Sutherland Square in Walworth. There are two

Newpin and new hope

Newpins in Northern Ireland, now functioning under
a different name, but there are six in Australia, when
Anne planted the seed at a conference she attended.

It is so wonderful to see people change and happy
children secure in the love of their mother, who now
listens to their needs instead of screaming; and they
now get a hug. As Andrea Pound so rightly said
'It is difficult to conceive of any other therapeutic
intervention, however skilled or intensive, which could
have achieved so much for so many in such a brief
span of time'. And it is not expensive to run. In fact
Newpin co-ordinators are competent Newpin mothers
trained especially for the job.

Suddenly, there was very disturbing news. Guy's
Health District and Lewisham were to be amalgamated.
I was told that my department would have to move to
Lewisham. The Health Education Officer in Lewisham
worked very differently from myself and one of us
would be appointed for the senior post. I was fifty-nine
and I regretfully decided to leave.

Chapter six
The boat

From Troubles of the World I Turn to Ducks
Ducks by F. W. Harvey

I was not ready to retire and I had become friendly with
the Principal of Southwark Adult Education Institute.
When I told him that I was leaving Guy's he suggested
that I become the Health Education Consultant at
Southwark Institute for ten hours a week, and was
funded by the Physical Education Department. He
also told me of the amazing history of the magnificent
building, which was built on three floors. It was very
light with large bay windows and attractively designed.
It had been purpose built in the 1930s as a pioneer
health centre by several doctors, the prime movers
being Dr Scott Williamson and Dr Pearse, and
became known as 'The Peckham Experiment'. Dr
Williamson realised that patients repeatedly returned
to his surgery with the same problems. Many were
depressed and malnourished. When the new building
opened the whole family within a small radius could
join for a small fee. They were all medically examined
on joining. It was found that a high percentage had
serious health problems and these people were
referred for treatment to their local doctor or hospital.

The boat

The health centre was open plan, light and airy, and centred around a swimming pool. There was a gym, theatre, cafeteria and room for other activities and workshops. It was run by the people themselves and the staff responded to the families' needs. The children would come in after school and the father after work. The families were given opportunities to expand their knowledge and potential. They did not have lectures but they could seek advice. Eventually there were so many projects, and one Christmas day they had a very successful Christmas party for eight hundred people. They paid a small fee for every activity they joined and this was additional to the small entrance fee. The farm at Bromley provided healthy food at a reasonable price. Also, there was a gift of land at Sissinghurst for holidays. The families became not just healthier but happier. Instead of sitting in their homes with nothing interesting to do their lives were changed by the community and the accessibility of activities. The government heard of the scheme but were in the process of setting up the National Health Service, which was for the treatment of disease, and of course the Health Centre was for the prevention of disease. It closed in 1939 because of the war. It opened briefly after the war and closed eventually in the 1950s. It was therefore very appropriate that I became the first Health Education Consultant in this historic building. I visited all the classes and found that there were some very committed people working in the Institute. The Breakthrough Trust was a charity for helping the deaf, and the branch in the Institute was run by an attractive, extremely deaf woman, who spoke excellent English. She told me of her plans for those deaf people who attended the institute. Cookery classes for those who were deaf were combined with those with normal hearing. She took a group of deaf people to the theatre for the first time. She said that their reaction to the experience was one of joy and opened up their silent world to new opportunities.

I decided to run a course to encourage good health using my health education contacts. The district dietician came, discussing healthy eating, and the head of sport in the Institute was only too pleased to talk about the importance of exercise. The Institute of Respiratory Medicine came with their machines to test the lung capacity of smokers, followed by a hospital pharmacist talking about herbs versus medicines, and then various experts came describing their form of alternative medicine. A hospital researcher into the menopause spoke of her research into the effects of Hormone Replacement Therapy. I held an exhibition for the staff, when their blood pressures were monitored and advice given on the prevention of heart disease. At the end of two years the Principal said that he now had the funding for a second sports tutor, and that was good news, but there was no funding for me and my job was over.

I had enjoyed my two years, but it was very different working for education after the health service. There was always a sense of urgency in the health service and in education it was more relaxed, but of course we were working with adults and not children. I attended yoga classes and swam in their lovely pool and continued these activities after I had left.

At this time Lionel's secretary was leaving and I decided to take her place. It was an interesting time for the future of the Lincoln, as the lease for the Lincoln Tower was ending, and the new rent proposals were beyond our financial means. I was able to re-organise the secretarial system and the filing cabinets in preparation for the appointment of our new business manager. He was a lawyer and a very good asset for the Lincoln. Indeed, he found our new premises in an attractive Mews in Clapham, which we were able to buy.

So many good things happened at about this time. Firstly, Fiona, my daughter, married her Pete whom she had met at Southampton University. They had both graduated in geophysical sciences, although Fiona returned two years later to take a degree in oceanography. They both worked for oil firms. Fiona translating the information from the field, and Pete in the field in charge of a workforce of two hundred in Bangladesh. They had become engaged in India in January and needed to be married in July when Pete was on leave. The only date for church and venue was the thirteenth. The sun shone and all was well and it was such a memorable occasion. A thunderstorm arrived at 10.30pm so we had a relatively early night, with the guests departing after the barbecue!

The boat

Lionel had been intrigued with a patient's well behaved Yorkshire terrier dog, which she brought to her session, and sat obediently on Lionel's desk. Lionel enthused and decided we should buy a Yorkshire terrier. We visited kennels and met four month old Monty. He was almost black in colour but was eventually gold with a silky coat. He was very intelligent, funny and brightened our lives.

At the same time we went to the Boat Show and met Tom McClean, a remarkable man, who had twice rowed across the Atlantic alone. He was brought up in an orphanage and eventually joined the S.A.S. After all his adventures he founded an outward bound centre in the Highlands. We bought Tom Mclean's fascinating book 'Rough Passage' in the front of which he wrote 'To Lionel with regards from the Lone Sailor' and he signed it together with a drawing of his sailing boat 'Giltspur'. After meeting Tom and exploring all the boats at the show we decided to have one ourselves. We found that a boat mortgage and a second-hand boat was a good option. We bought an excellent boat found for us by the Chiswick boatyard. It was a twin-engine Seamaster and we moored it at Chiswick Quay Marina. The first time we viewed the boat we took little Monty who promptly fell into the water. We had no means of drying him so we put him in a low oven to dry off. Hot dog!! We found that the name of our boat had been incorrectly spelt. It should have been Inchmahome, where the Monteiths' had originally lived. The name put on the boat was Inch-ma-Home! There were often very

The boat

surprising names on the boats, the most memorable one being 'Cirrhosis of the River'. This was very apt, as there was no curb on drinking and driving!

It was a tidal marina so the gates would only open at high tide. On our first attempt to go out Lionel fell overboard. The Marina was deep and Lionel could not swim. He clung on to the ropes and had some painful rope burns. The local coastguard was a woman called Molly. She happened to be nearby and told Lionel to strip to his pants and she would dry his clothes. She brought brandy for shock and towels to warm him. The second time we decided to go out the keel became hooked on a buoy in the marina and we therefore hired a diver to unhook us.

The people in the marina were very friendly and of course we had now joined the fraternity of the boat people. There was the couple who had sold their house and were readying their boat to live in the Mediterranean. One man owned a beautiful wooden launch which had been at Dunkirk. He asked Molly the way to France. She said 'You turn left and when you reach the Channel you turn right'. On the way there he thought he should check his direction asking another boat. He was told that if he continued on his present course he would be in Stavanger in the morning!

Lionel and Tom McClean

Our boat, Inchmahome

The boat

The following spring on the boat we decided to go upriver. It was early March, and the sun was setting as we cruised along. Lionel said that he could smell burning and one of the engines stopped, and a little while later the second engine became silent. Here we were, on the very wide river by Kew Bridge and without power. We lowered the anchor and waited, hoping for another boat. Suddenly, the bronzed and confident river police arrived and towed us back to the Marina. We learnt that the boatyard had 'winterised' the boat, thereby removing all the cooling water for the engines which were burnt out. It was a very costly mistake due to our ignorance. The next winter we 'winterised' the boat ourselves.

A few months later we went to the Royal Academy summer exhibition. We were soon attracted to a glowing sunset oil painting of the Thames by Kew Bridge, by William Bowyer, a member of the Royal Academy. We knew we had to have it. Lionel tentatively looked at the price and we bought it, and it is still hanging on my wall, reminding me of the day when the engines burnt out.

In January, we applied to the river authority for a boat race mooring by the finishing post at Chiswick Bridge. In order to catch the tide for the following day we had to moor on the Thames the evening before. Otherwise, owing to the tides we would not have been able to leave the marina. The first time we did this, it was a wild March evening, pouring with rain, a gale

The boat

blowing and six foot high waves. We arrived at the pier on the river, and with our boat hooks tried to pass our ropes through the rusty chains. I was desperate, as the boat heaved and I cried with tears streaming down my cheeks. I felt that I was up against the power of nature and then I fell on the tarpaulin cover of the boat moored on the other side of the narrow walkway. Lionel came to my rescue and we hooked up. Our friend, a former Cunard captain, appropriately dressed in his yellow weatherproofs had moored behind us! 'It is so rough, I shall have to take you to shore separately' he said. I was so glad to be on dry land again. I squelched into my seat in the car and steamed, as we put the heating on high and drove home.

It was worth it as we watched the end of the race vigorously ringing our boat bell, drinking champagne and having a party. It was astonishing to see the speed at which the Oxford and Cambridge crews sped by.

One lovely summer's day with Fiona and Pete on board we decided to cruise to the newly built Thames Barrier. We started out at 8am passing under Chiswick Bridge and following the route of the boat race. We took photographs of the underside of the bridges which were all different and some were very beautiful. As we passed Traitors' Gate leading to the Tower of London we thought of those who had made that final journey. It was a thrill passing the Houses of Parliament, the Royal Palace at Greenwich, and then on to the then old deserted warehouses until in the distance gleamed the

The boat

new Thames Barrier. There were huge notices warning us not to pass through the barrier, which we ignored, whilst admiring the towering silver metal architecture above us.

On our return journey we moored at Greenwich and black swans surrounded the boat hoping for food. Fiona and Pete left us at the newly built festival pier. As we neared Hammersmith we became stuck on a mudbank. A small boat passed by and offered to help and towed us to deeper water. We could not enter our marina because of the low tide and anchored up river.

The banks of the river changed with the seasons and abounded with wild flowers, and now and again we saw motionless herons and the cormorants. It was very relaxing watching the bird life and the activity on the river. I am reminded of a poem entitled 'Ducks' by F. W. Harvey.

From troubles of the world
I turn to ducks
Beautiful comical things
Sleeping or curled
Their heads beneath white wings
By water cool.

We found the tidal marina very inhibiting and decided to go to the non-tidal river beyond Tenterden, at

The boat

Thames Ditton. I wished that I had been able to paint then, as I can now. When cooking in the galley one day I watched a female grebe pass by ferrying her chicks on her back. Then there were the Canada geese flying black against the sunset, and at night the mist rising on the water with the moon giving ghostly shadows. One night when moored at Teddington the little goblin lights of anglers glimmered along the banks. In the evening we would moor at Hampton Court and walk through the deserted gardens after closing time. Monty, our little Yorkie, loved the boat and was friends with a great Dane who would peer in the window to see if Monty was available.

Although we had our adventures, life on the river was very peaceful. Lionel enjoyed being the 'captain', wearing his captain's hat and having 'fun' in the bilge. I was not over enthusiastic negotiating the locks, leaping up or down to secure the ropes, but our family and friends enjoyed the river experience. Meanwhile, I felt restless as I needed a job. I read in the newspaper that a certain M.P. biologist, by the name of Theresa Gorman, had founded an organisation to help menopausal women, called The Amarant Trust. I read the article with interest and decided to write and offer my services which were quickly accepted.

The main consultant was Malcolm Whitehead, a gynaecologist from King's College Hospital who ran the clinics. The phone calls to the clinic were continuous and I suggested that perhaps I could run an answer phone from home.

This idea was accepted and I was very busy, and even had calls from Kenya and Malta. I was used to taking histories when I ran the antenatal clinic and I did this with every caller. There was no textbook to which I could refer and I learnt so much from the patients' reactions to their H.R.T. medication. I ran the advice line for approximately seven years until I was asked by a pharmaceutical firm to train three nurses to run an advice line. This had been organised by an Amarant doctor who lived at Crawley where the advice line would be based. I was then seventy five years of age!

Two years after Fiona and Pete were married, Catherine, my granddaughter was born, and two and a half years later was followed by Christopher. Catherine loved the boat and we bought her a very expensive life jacket which was very necessary for a lively toddler. Christopher was one year old when he last came to the boat, as the next year Inchmahome was sold and a new phase of my life was about to begin.

Chapter seven

Bereavement

So we'll go no more a-roving

Lord Byron

One cold day in January 1991 my husband, Lionel Monteith, had a heart attack and died. In the morning I was a wife and by the evening a widow. My great concern was Lionel's patients and the sensitive task of informing them of Lionel's death. Also, I needed to phone the Lincoln to arrange to offer alternative therapies to these bereaved patients.

Pete, my son-in-law arranged for his parents to travel from Kings Lynn to Orpington to look after his two children. This enabled my daughter, Fiona to stay the night. We had experienced such care at King's College Hospital, where Lionel died, that I wrote a letter thanking them all. The ambulance staff, the doctors and nursing staff were all so efficient. We collected the death certificate from the hospital and then went on to the registrars to register the death. Those registering births and marriages were also waiting in the same room. Of course we are born, married and die, and it was a salutary experience.

Bereavement

When Fiona had left I contacted Jean Sergeant, the wife of Howard, Lionel's oldest friend, who had died, and asked her if she could come and help me. She assisted in the writing of Lionel's obituaries for *The Times* and the *Daily Telegraph*.

I phoned Lionel's sister, Sybil, who lived in Alderney. She left immediately and was with me the next day.

I contacted a close psychoanalyst friend who lived in the next road, who realising my distress said 'Come and see me at seven o'clock on Friday morning'. I felt overwhelmed at the immediate response and the love and kindness shown to me, which has continued, and I am so thankful.

Lionel's diary held a list of his patients with their appointments and they had to be contacted and alternative therapists found. It was such a shock for them and a bereavement.

I could not sleep and my adrenaline was flowing as I had so much to organise.

I visited the funeral director whose name was Mr Sleep. His glamorous assistant sat elegantly on a high stool painting her nails. The situation was bizarre. Mr Sleep lived up to his name leaving the presiding Minister, Keith Havers, at the City Temple, and drove us on to the crematorium, where another vicar kindly took the service.

Bereavement

I had chosen a date for the funeral convenient for the Lincoln therapists, and now I had to choose a Church. I decided on the City Temple in Holborn, where Lionel had preached in the past, and which had been Rev. Leslie Weatherhead's church.

Then there was the music. A Lincoln analyst had a son who was a famous flautist. I contacted her and she arranged an organist and two soloists from the Guildhall School of Music.

Keith Havers was a university colleague of Lionel's and I asked him if he would be the presiding minister, and he readily agreed. We were now almost ready for the printing of the order of service and Jean had a relative who was an editor and he agreed to print it. This service was going to be a celebration of Lionel's life and I needed an appropriate hat, so Fiona, my sister-in-law Sybil and I all went hat shopping.

There were all the friends and relations to contact, two of them travelling from Exeter and three from Norwich.

The organist was inspired, playing Elgar's Nimrod, as the coffin was carried up the aisle and everyone stood until the music ended. The rich music, the words of appreciation of Lionel's life by Keith Havers and Anton Obholzer, the reading by Jean of one of Lionel's poems, the singing of the two hymns, especially the hymn 'Forth in Thy name O Lord I go', made the service moving and memorable. The funeral director and his team were ready to carry the coffin to the hearse when the triumphant strains of Jeremiah Clarke's 'Trumpet Voluntary' rang out and all stood as before. There were over one hundred people at the service. They were relatives, friends, therapists and patients.

When I reached home after the funeral I found flowers awaiting me on the doorstep from one of Lionel's former patients. I was so moved.

I had left a message on the answerphone of my Menopause Advice Line stating that my service would resume in two weeks, that is two weeks after Lionel's death. It was good that I had other people to help who were in need.

I went to see Gerald Wooster, the psychoanalyist, who had offered to see me on Friday morning before the funeral. He had been a good friend to Lionel. I sobbed for an hour. Gerald saw me once a week for a year at a more convenient time. The bereavement counselling was so helpful.

The Lincoln was Lionel's life and I felt that I should help the organisation. I was still in a hyperactive state. I thought the Lincoln should have a portrait of their founder. I always loved the work of the R.A. artist William Bowyer. I rang him and he agreed to paint an oil portrait which still hangs at the Lincoln. When I visited his studio lined with his arresting paintings he asked me to turn around. There was Lionel's picture on the easel and the eyes looked directly at me. It was just as if he was alive again.

Lionel had been a poet before I knew him, and was recognised as the editor of his magazines of Commonwealth poetry. He had published poems of very famous poets, one of them being the Australian, Judith Wright. He had met Dylan Thomas, Stephen Spender, H. E. Bates and others. He, with Howard Sergeant, founded a weekly poetry reading at The Greyhound Pub in Dulwich Village. Some time before Lionel died he was interviewed by a Canadian author, Bruce Meyer. Bruce was interested in writing Howard Sergeant's biography, for by now Howard was recognised as a poet of some standing. Bruce wanted Howard's history from Lionel's perspective and also to publish some of Lionel's poems. I contacted Bruce and asked him to select some of Lionel's poems to publish in a booklet, and also to write an introduction. I phoned Danny Abse, an old friend, and a distinguished poet, and asked if he could write the forward. Howard's wife Jean edited the book entitled 'And so he went Sailing', a line from one of Lionel's poems.

Every year we held a party under a canopy in the Lincoln Mews courtyard and I decided that this would be a good time to launch the poetry book. I would charge five pounds for the book and give the proceeds to the Lincoln, for the Lionel Monteith Memorial Fund, which would give financial help to new students.

Bereavement

As Lionel's portrait was completed I thought it apt for our granddaughter Catherine to help me unveil it. She was three and a half years old and looked engagingly sweet with her long blond hair and dressed in a blue velvet dress. I was overwhelmed by the occasion and found it difficult to make my speech.

It was after Lionel died that the executive committee realised the extent of his work and dedication. He *was* the Lincoln Clinic. Committees were hurriedly formed to deal with the allocation of patients and other administrative functions. Today there are at least eight committees dealing with the Lincoln administration.

I was determined to raise money for the Lincoln, as we were a charity attempting to keep the cost of therapy at affordable levels. When Christmas came I made ten Christmas cakes to sell for ten pounds at the Christmas concert I had organised at St Olaves, Pepys' old church in the city. I had a friend who belonged to a professional choir who agreed to sing. There had been a wedding the day before and the church looked beautiful, decorated with ivy and white roses and lit by candles. I sold all my cakes and made one hundred pounds.

One of Lionel's patients was connected with the Guildhall School of Music and agreed to help with a Valentine concert, which he arranged at St Giles Church at the Barbican with an amazing saxophonist as a soloist. We supplied white wine, together with an artificial rose. Real roses were just too expensive. I cannot remember the entrance fee. The saxophonist was inspired and we clapped enthusiastically as he played, marching up and down the aisles.

Our business manager was leaving and was being replaced by a woman from Scotland who had nowhere to live. Her name was Norah Smith, and having met her I invited her to live with me. This was an ideal arrangement as she was training to be a Jungian therapist. She could use Lionel's consulting room to see patients. Also, it was company for me although a little bizarre as she was about to be married on 1st April. She travelled to Scotland every two weeks to be with her new husband.

How did I feel as all this was happening? Outwardly, I appeared to look as if I was coping but I was living on two levels. The pain was hammering away underneath. I decided to keep fully occupied. I would learn to paint, and joined a Bromley Adult Education course. The oil painting class was run by a superb teacher and artist, and I have never looked back and now sell my paintings. The other class I joined was quilt making. Again, I was fortunate in having a teacher from the Royal College of Needlework. She helped me design the quilt which I made from all Lionel's ties. He never threw a tie away. I unpicked them and ironed them. All the navy and dark ties formed the edge. There were ties of silk, rayon and cotton. There were flower power

ties and those of all colours. There were ties from the
family and it has become an heirloom.

My family were very supportive. When I was staying
with Fiona, one morning my small granddaughter,
Catherine crept into my bed. I was crying and she said
'Don't cry Grandma, I will be your friend'. I have never
forgotten her words and she is now twenty five and is
still my friend.

I went on holiday with them to my beloved Norfolk,
Wales and Devon and it was a delight to be with my
two small grandchildren, give them breakfast and take
them for a walk, to give their parents a good rest. We
would parade through the woods with me singing
'Come follow, follow me' and I would be leading
and the 'little dears' following. But still the pain of
bereavement was there. I wondered when I would be
really happy again. It took nearly three years.

When Hamish was told of his father's death he
showed no emotion. He came to the funeral and was
achingly calm. However, he was far from well, being
very restless and forever thirsty. His daytime activities
were boring and his hostel far from ideal. I asked
Gerald Wooster whether he could help. He said that a
Professor of Mental Health had recently retired from St
George's Hospital and could possibly be of assistance.
Her name was Joan Bicknell. She was able to access
Hamish's records from the Maudsley Hospital, and
found that he had been diagnosed by Lorna Wing

as having Asperger's syndrome. At last I knew what was wrong with my son. She changed his medication and gave me a list of possible places where he could live. I chose The Rare Breeds Centre, organised by the Canterbury Oast Trust, near Tenterden. The farm was run mainly by staff for the residents with Down's syndrome and some with other disabilities. They also have a restaurant in Rye staffed by those with Down's syndrome. One of the criteria which so impressed me, was that although disabled, the facilities should be first class, and they are. Hamish resisted the idea of change and I had to arrive unexpectedly to take him to the farm. They were so good to him and eventually he was looking after the pigs!

Hamish had an excellent social worker, and he, with Joan Bicknell, came to the Southwark Council meeting for the funding of this project. I had also had an interview with our local Egyptian counsellor. He understood the situation, as his brother was a psychotherapist, and he gave me his support. Eventually the funding was allowed and has continued to the end of his life.

A nursing friend of mine, Diana Cawston, had retired at fifty to spend summers at her house in a small Greek village. In 1992, she asked me to come for a two week holiday. Diana originally went to Greece as a volunteer in her twenties when her naval husband had tragically died. Greece was in great need of help after the Second World War and Diana formed lasting Greek friendships, one of which was instrumental in helping Diana to buy a one roomed family house in a village by the sea. Through the years Diana has gradually added to it and it now has sanitation, electricity and running water. It is now a charming villa with a large garden and fruit trees. As someone else was caring for Hamish and I could relax I flew to Preveza, the airport consisting of a few sheds. Diana was there to meet me and we drove to the tiny village of Ayios Tomas.

There was a kind of store and a church. Diana's house was charming with bougainvillea, hydrangeas and geraniums, a large stretch of lawn and screened from the sea by thick bamboos. That night we sat on the veranda listening to the nightingales and watching the fireflies with their fairy lights flitting around. The nights were quite noisy with the farms' guard dogs barking and the chugging of the sardine fishing boats setting off from the harbour nearby. The day's routine was quite undemanding. When the feral cats knew we were stirring, about half a dozen of them would appear at the back door with their foot long tails as straight as rulers.

There were always kittens which Diana nurtured and loved. Large tortoises would appear out of the undergrowth and Diana would always be snipping away at the grass with shears, but now she has a 'Flymo' and also a neighbour who willingly cuts her grass for her. After breakfast we waited awhile and went swimming in the bay at the end of the garden.

Bereavement

We took ice cream tubs to gather the spiny sea
urchins, and also stones for the garden paths.

The sea was deserted and the water warm. After a
swim we would have a cold water shower under the
lemon trees. Then it was coffee. Lunch was salad with
feta cheese and yoghurt washed down with wine.
The afternoon was siesta time and I lay on a lounger
under the trees covered by a protective sheet and had
a snooze. Diana brought tea at four when we talked
and had a meal. On Wednesdays we caught the bus
to Preveza. The goatherd would be leading his flock
to their pasture with their bells ringing softly. The bus
would be full of very well behaved schoolchildren with
their freshly brushed black shining hair. When we
arrived we went to the bakers to buy delicious cheese
turnovers, fresh from the oven. We bought a long
drink of fresh lemon juice and sat eating our breakfast
at a nearby restaurant. We then went shopping, the
last shop being the off-licence where the wine was in
huge barrels where Diana refilled her bottles. She left
her shopping by the counter where she said it would
be safe. She said that the Greeks were very honest
and they are. I bought a large straw hat and visited a
shop owned by friends of Diana's where they made
beautiful olive wood bowls. I bought a mustard pot and
a wonderfully carved pear for Diana.

On another day we visited the Roman ruins of nearby
Heraclion. The wonderfully complete Roman mosaic
floor was only covered by old sacking which we

carefully lifted and gazed with awe on this ancient work of art. We saw Cleopatra's bath (there seem to be quite a few of these scattered about. She must have been a clean lady!). We saw where St Paul had preached and a sculpture of his face in a nearby museum. Diana spoke Greek which eased our way. We had a sweet black coffee with her widowed neighbour who was dressed in traditional black, whose son was called Odysseus. It was a lovely holiday and I fell in love with Greece. When I returned home I painted my first oil painting from a photograph of light through olive trees, with white camomile growing beneath the trees. We had just picked twenty pounds of tomatoes to make chutney and I took the photograph on the way back. The painting is hanging above my fireplace.

In spite of all this activity I still had an aching heart. I knew I needed to make plans for the future. I needed to move to a town with civic pride, like Norwich. I chose Tunbridge Wells where I also had ties. Lionel had lived there until he was nine. I had organised Health Education conferences at the nearby Salomon's Centre. I did not know the significance of the choice I was making of going to live in Tunbridge Wells. Our lives depend so often on which road we take.

Chapter eight

Friends in Australia

The Pleasures of Friendship are exquisite
Stevie Smith

I had never wanted to live in London but I had done so since I was nineteen. I would have preferred to live in my beloved Norfolk but both my children lived in Kent and so Tunbridge Wells was a good choice.

Firstly, I had to prepare the house ready for sale. The loft was full of twenty-five years of the family's discarded clutter. There was still a collection of childhood toys, old school books, old saucepans and kitchen equipment. In those days there were no charity shops, only jumble sales. The collection of Lionel's theological books were gratefully received by the Salvation Army training college which was nearby. I had a cleaner who was a Jehovah's witness. She said that her husband would clear the loft after my children had rescued their childhood belongings. I needed to dispose of our large book collection. I had help with both these problems and was eventually ready to put the house on the market. Again, help arrived. Gerald Wooster had a psychoanalyst friend who needed to move closer to the centre of London and she bought the house.

I needed to choose where to live. I wanted to live near my children, be close to the country and move to a town like Norwich which had civic pride. I chose Tunbridge Wells. Lionel had often spoken about it with enthusiasm, and I had often been to conferences at Salomon's Centre at Speldhurst, near Tunbridge Wells. Tunbridge Wells was half an hour from Orpington where Fiona and family lived and one hour from St Mary's bay where Hamish was happily settled. I chose a delightful Victorian detached house in Tunbridge Wells. The present owners, with their three children, intended moving to a much larger house. The wife was half Dutch and the husband half Italian and an opera singer. I had an excess of furniture and offered it to them which they gladly accepted. When I moved, the furniture for the larger house was off-loaded first, and then mine for my new house.

My new home had once been a shop and had large storage sheds at the back which needed demolishing. Lionel had once been a quantity surveyor and always said that it was wise to employ a builder through a builder's surveyor, which I duly did. There were quite a few alterations to be done, also the building of a conservatory, the creating of a back garden and decorating throughout. The builder had been a quantity surveyor and he and his team were an excellent choice. They did an excellent job and when the alterations were complete I invited them to a barbecue. I did not know anyone in Tunbridge Wells and it was good to have their company.

On the day after I moved I was standing in the front garden when a voice asked if I had just arrived. I looked up to see a military looking man standing at the gate. He said 'I am David McNair, welcome to Tunbridge Wells'. I was flabbergasted to have this warm greeting after living in London where neighbours seemed to be icily indifferent. When I went to buy the paper, again I was greeted as I walked up the hill by people saying 'Good morning'. I felt I belonged.

I was within walking distance of all the shops. This was such a change from London where specialist items were only available in Oxford Street. Here, everything was on hand. A large and wooded park was only five minutes away which was convenient for Monty, my Yorkshire terrier's walks. I even had a bus stop outside the house which would take me to Sainsbury's but I was still driving my mini.

I imagined that this was to be my home until I died.

I now set about making friends. I joined the U3A (University of the Third Age), and went to their monthly meeting, and attended play-reading and poetry groups. I applied to become a bereavement counsellor at the local hospice. The second meeting did not go well as I burst into tears and was told that I had yet to deal with my own bereavement first. I started working in the British Heart Foundation charity shop where I made friends. At Christmas I invited my neighbours to a party. I had a Zimmer frame and buggies outside the front door. We had such a merry time. Then I had the idea of starting a U3A scrabble group which lasted several years and was a great success. All this time I was still running the Menopause Advice Line. In September, I joined an Adult Education watercolour class and again had an excellent tutor. At last my bereavement burden was lifting and I enjoyed Christmas for the first time in three years.

The family came in February and we celebrated my seventieth birthday. Then Diana asked me to stay with her again in Greece. I had always coloured my hair brown but this time I mistook the colour and to my horror when I looked in the mirror my hair was jet black. Diana said that I should not worry as the Greeks all had black hair! Before I left for Greece I found a 'dog sitter' for Monty. She was also a painter and as I admired her watercolours she told me of the Tunbridge Wells Art Society and showed me their interesting programme. When I returned from holiday I joined the Society and soon I was on the committee as Membership Secretary.

Marjorie, a close friend of mine who had been baby sitter for my children when in West Kensington, was ill in Charing Cross Hospital. She said that she would like to be discharged to Tunbridge Wells. She had had a tragic life and I was her only friend. She was then eighty five and she had been a smoker. She was on continuous oxygen. She wore a mask and the oxygen was always bubbling away as I visited her twice weekly. She was so thin that she was even unable to have a bath. She remained amazingly cheerful and enjoyed being looked after. She said she had never experienced care as a child and was making up for the deprivation!

At this time I was thinking about visiting Australia. My father had lived in Australia as a 'Jackaroo' for five years, before I was born, and he told me how he had baked cakes in the ground, sheared sheep and ridden on horseback long miles in the outback in Queensland.

After five years he returned to England and joined the Royal Flying Corps. I arranged a visit to Australia for seven weeks in the Autumn, staying with Jim and Anne Stewart who lived in Toowoomba, in Queensland, about one hundred miles from Brisbane. Jim was a doctor and had come to England to train as a psychotherapist, having met and been inspired by Leslie Weatherhead. He envisaged working at the City Temple's Psychotherapy Clinic. We had met at the City Temple. We spent most of our free time with them. They already had two children and when Anne had her third baby I was present and gave Peter, their new baby, his first bath. Anne became very homesick and Jim reluctantly returned to Australia with his psychotherapy training incomplete. We were devastated and we missed them so much.

Anne was very excited about my trip and had planned an itinerary. I was fortunate in having friends in Adelaide, Melbourne and Sydney.

Jim and Anne's house, Toowoomba, Australia

I flew by Singapore airlines with the immaculate and stunningly beautiful Asian stewardesses to look after me. We were given blankets, pillows, socks and toothbrushes. After signing the entry form on arrival at Singapore, the airport seemed deserted. I had been told that I would be met. I eventually found a counter and a friendly courier and was instructed to take a taxi to the hotel, where the driver would be remunerated. It was so hot and humid that I stripped and stood in front of the air conditioner, drinking iced water from the thermos. I flung myself on the bed and fell into a dreamless sleep.

After a luscious breakfast of tropical fruit and cereal I took a taxi to the botanical gardens. I noticed that most of the women had paper-like sunshades. I walked slowly to the insistent sound of the cicadas and marvelled at the statues strategically placed among the leafy trees, and the fan-like tracery of the palm trees, and then I came to the delicacy of the orchid garden. I had never experienced such humidity and found it very difficult to walk slowly back to my hotel. Opposite the hotel was a Chinese temple with women bathing their hands in the smoke rising from the fires. The street adjoining the temple was lined with Chinese shops. After lunch I took a taxi to the river and a boat trip to various landmarks, including the famous Raffles hotel, the scene of many a scandal, especially when owned by the British before the war.

I next visited the impressive glittering shopping centre which seemed to include every well known western shop and was sparkling and spotlessly clean.

After the evening meal I prepared to catch the all night Quantus flight to Brisbane. I had not seen my friends for forty years but I recognised them instantly. They were just older and greyer as I was too. It is amazing how with true friends the relationship resumes almost seamlessly.

Their spreading clapboard house was built on stilts to withstand the various invading insects. The garden was colourful with plants we would normally grow indoors. Anne loved her garden and watering the plants was her first priority. She had been brought up on a sheep farm one hundred miles from the nearest town. She and her two sisters were educated by their mother until it was time for them to attend boarding school. When we had breakfast on the 'deck' we overlooked the inviting blue swimming pool, the pale mauve of the jacaranda tree and the blue distance of the Gold Coast. The bird calls were mainly sharp squawks, whistles and bubbly sounds. There was of course, the kookaburra. One morning Anne said 'Can you hear that sound? That is a kookaburra learning to laugh'.

We would walk every evening marvelling at the changing evening light on the mountains, and hearing the red and green parrots chattering in the trees. At night the furry possums danced on the roof.

Anne played tennis and at one of her tennis parties I was asked if I would like to see their 'Joey'. I was introduced to 'Roo', a fully grown kangaroo, with large melting, long lashed eyes lying in a basket beside a golden retriever. Roo had been hand reared after her mother was killed. Anne was also an artist and the house was charming. At Christmas it expanded to accommodate her ever growing family of sixteen plus.

Friends in Australia

After a week we went whale watching at Hervey Bay.
Nothing is 'near' in Australia and we travelled nearly
four hundred miles, occasionally meeting a shiny metal
puffing pantechnicon. We stayed in attractive chalets
and the next day caught a boat, with Fraser Island
on our right, an island totally made of sand. There are
rules about whale watching. Boats are required to
stay at a certain distance from the sightings. It was a
magical moment when we saw the plume of water in
the air and the rolling massive body of the whale – just
like David Attenborough's experience, but not as good.

Then on to the hippie centre of Byron Bay to meet Jed,
Jim and Anne's eldest son. Jed lived in a commune
near the beach and practised alternative medicine.
When we arrived we were each offered a massage,
which was rejuvenating. I also had my first experience
of Reiki. Jed's hand held above my back radiated a
soothing warmth which was very pleasant.

When lunch was ready we sat in the floor in a circle,
joined hands and closed eyes. Lunch was vegetarian
and delicious, eaten to the soft hypnotic music of Enya.

The next day we were sitting on the deserted beach
at Byron Bay when a horse drawn wagon appeared
driven by a gnome like man with a long white beard. The
wagon was weirdly decorated and labelled 'Art Shop'.
He was accompanied by a darkly handsome rider on
a magnificent horse. We rubbed our eyes in disbelief.
When we returned to our chalet a gnome like man with

a long white beard was wheeling a wheelbarrow. We wondered if we would soon see Snow White!

The next day we were on the way to the top of a mountain at Binna Burra and the Mountain Lodge in Lamington National Park. We passed several forest fires smoking in the distance. It was dark when we arrived but our sturdy green tents were well lit. Little animals like small kangaroos were munching the grass outside the tent. When we gathered the next morning there were eight of us, including two children. Binna Burra was a favourite holiday place for the family. Today we were visiting the eel pool in the dark, silent depths of the ancient rainforest. We negotiated huge roots and vines and the narrow path twisted its way down and down. It was like stepping back in time in a primordial silence. The eel pool was surrounded by huge rocks and some light glimmered through the trees. The children and some of the braver ones plunged into the ice cold water.

It was a long and difficult climb to the top, over stones and roots, when suddenly I heard Jim's voice, 'How's your angina, Mary?' As we climbed up to the light, all was silent, when suddenly there was a loud cat-like cry. We met a warden who told us that it was the cry of a cat bird. We were exhausted when we reached the top. Jim's daughter Mary volunteered to climb to the Lodge and get the car. It was wonderful to climb in and to know we would soon be in our tent. When we met for a picnic that evening in Jim's tent, with the Billy can bubbling on the gas stove, Jed playing softly on his

Binna Burra, Queensland, Australian rainforest

guitar, and the loving warmth of friendship around me,
I was moved to tears.

The next day Jim treated us all to a sumptuous meal in
the lodge, with red and green parrots peering in at the
window. It was our last day and we set off on the long
homeward drive.

We went to lovely parks and gardens, seeing large
colourful butterflies and different types of trees.
The gum trees with their grey white trunks were so
attractive. We visited a nature reserve where sleepy
koalas lounged in the trees. As their diet is mainly of
bamboo shoots they have very little energy.

119

I reluctantly left Toowoomba and my dear friends, and flew to Adelaide. As I was over sixty I paid a special reduced rate for the flight. I was going to stay with Jenny Kinmont, sister of Meredith Daneman, one of the glamorous ballet dancers who had spent Christmas with us in 1960. Jenny was a skilled photographer and she and Merry had published a book of poems in 1964 illustrated with children's photographs entitled 'I am the Green Grass'. Two of the photographs were of my then three year old daughter, Fiona.

Jenny had returned to Australia and Merry had married the actor Paul Daneman. She had subsequently written a few novels. I had arranged to visit Merry to find out Jenny's address. Merry was living in a house by the Thames at Putney. She was still beautiful and we chatted, catching up on the years since we last met. Merry was in the throes of writing Margot Fonteyn's biography and was finding it very difficult. Merry's elder daughter Sophie, was an opera singer. She had sung at Covent Garden and Aldeburgh and she was to sing in the Opera House whilst I was in Sydney.

We had always been very fond of Jenny who loved the children. I remember her seeing snow for the first time, when she rushed into the garden dancing with delight. Jenny was very surprised and pleased to hear from me and arranged to meet me at Adelaide airport. I recognised her immediately with her wide smile and snow white curly hair like a thick halo.

Adelaide, in New South Wales, was very different from Queensland. There were less people and the streets were wide and straight. It was quite British with a portrait of the stout and small eyed Henry the Eighth in the art gallery, with other members of the British royal family. We went to a free Bach lunchtime concert which was not very well attended, and visited the impressive Aboriginal Centre with its dream time designs. I bought material for a tablecloth with a brown, white and golden design.

I saw my first pelican on the beach in Adelaide. I also saw the blazing sun sink suddenly below the horizon from the top of the rotating restaurant overlooking the beach. I was to meet Jenny in Sydney where she had tickets for Sophie's concert just before I went home.

My next stop was Melbourne, where I was to stay with John and Angela Masterton. They were friends of ours in West Kensington where John was the doctor at U.C.H. who introduced Lionel to the Psychiatric Department. Angela and I had met in the local park with our prams. She had been a nurse at Great Ormond Street Hospital. We soon became friends. They had emigrated with their four children to Australia, and John was Chair of Surgery at Monash University in Melbourne. They lived in an attractive two storey house with a luxuriant garden and I had the use of the whole of the first floor. They were so good to me, taking me to so many interesting places and I was pleased to find that my British National Trust card was accepted in Australia. They lived in a delightful tree lined suburb and we drove along to the town centre, passing the exotic railway station which was designed by Lutyens and meant for Delhi!

The doorway of the Melbourne Art Gallery looked impassable at first glance as sheets of water were in continuous flow over the entrance. The art gallery was light and airy, and the arresting pictures portrayed the Australian sunlight. The first floor ceiling was of stunning stained glass, and cushions were provided to lie and view the jewel like designs.

We next visited the large Botanical Gardens with fruit bats hanging from trees like small black shiny umbrellas. The gardens housed a vast collection of Aboriginal medicinal plants which were a source of interest to pharmaceutical companies.

On the next day boarding a large Land Rover we first visited John and Angela's married daughter in a wood where they had built themselves a beautiful wooden home with large plate glassed windows.

Then we went on to Ballarat, the old gold mining town which has been preserved as it was one hundred years ago with cobbled streets and shops selling vintage sweets and groceries. We went down a gold mine where streaks of gold were visible on the walls. The mining was done by hard pressed Chinese miners who often died of silicosis. We went on a ride on a large stage coach and I chose to sit on top and was nearly thrown, as the six horses started over the rough cobbled streets. In the evening John took us to dinner at a superb restaurant. What a day!

I phoned Helga Coulter who had trained as a psychotherapist at the Lincoln, and she invited me to dinner. She was so pleased to see me as I was a direct link with the Lincoln. Her house and garden were lovely and we spent an interesting evening talking about her work and aspirations.

My next and last stop was Sydney where I stayed with one of Jenny's friends. Sydney was a busy metropolis. I took two trips around the harbour and was looking forward to the evening performance at the Opera House whose massive shell like structure dominates the harbour. The interior was spacious and the acoustics excellent. Sophie's clear soprano voice soared away with such clarity. She was the principal soloist in Rameau's 'Les Grands Motets' and received a standing ovation. Jenny was going to Sophie's next performance in Canberra but I opted to go on a trip to the blue mountains.

I saw my first Aborigine, complete with painted face and body playing a didgeridoo. I felt sorry for him as he looked so out of place, and it was so demeaning as he was doing this to earn money. I did not remember much about this trip except the stunning mountain scenery.

Friends in Australia

My flight to Heathrow was overnight. I was able to lie down, I took a sleeping tablet and slept.

Australia was a wonderful experience which I treasure and like to remember, and I still keep in touch with my Australian friends Jim and Anne. Jim is ninety this year!

Chapter nine
New love

Yes, yours my Love is the right human face
From *The Confirmation* by Edwin Muir

It took time to adjust after Australia and Christmas was imminent. In January, I went to Adult Education to resume my watercolour classes. I was allocated to a class run by a man and of course there were more male students in the class. On my first day I noticed another student who was obviously new. He flashed me a smile and I was smitten. We became friends and then he joined the Art Society. Eventually we became lovers, and this week we have been married fourteen years, which have passed so quickly. We have so much in common, yet we are so different, but we complement one another. My husband is Norman William White but I call him Jay, after the 'J' in 'Just William'.

Jay had been a managing director of a firm called VG Electronics, designing and making electronic equipment, which was exported worldwide. He is a Fellow of the Institute of Engineering Technology and had been made a Fellow of the Royal Television Society for his contribution to television engineering and they also had given gave him an award for his outstanding contribution to television engineering in 1974. This award was presented by the Duke of Edinburgh. Jay will hate all this information written about him. He is so modest. I took some time to learn all these facts. He has a kind, honest face and kingfisher blue eyes, and is a man of great charm. Besides which I really value his wise judgement. He has travelled widely being a trouble shooter for other television companies, in Israel, Japan, Hong Kong, and behind the Iron Curtain. He has so many stories of his travels. He is over six feet tall and he towered over the Japanese in the underground. When he alighted he could not find the exit because the signs were in Japanese.

Our marriage, 18th July 2000, with our witnesses Peter Howarth and Christine Churchward

New love

When I met Jay I did not know all this. He was just an artist struggling to learn the watercolour technique. He had come from a loving family. His father was a great inspiration to him, encouraging him in his teens to build a radio and a television set. He had a brother, who, sadly, at three months caught measles and was made profoundly deaf.

It is extraordinary that my first husband was analytical of human emotions, and that Jay is analytical of the origins of the Earth, especially quantum physics. He has alerted me to the beauty and symmetry of the smallest particle, as David Attenborough has demonstrated the marvels of the smallest insect. Jay has taught me so much. He has a love and understanding of music and has introduced me to opera. We enjoy the same television programmes especially Wimbledon tennis.

Jay taught me chess. You see it is possible to teach an old dog new tricks and now I am computer literate (almost). We discuss and never quarrel. We laugh a lot and daily voice our love for one and other. I never knew I could fall so completely in love like a teenager, in my Seventies and he is so romantic.

When we married, and were looking for witnesses, I asked Peter my hairdresser and Chris who washed my hair, if they would oblige. It was a beautiful sunny day when we met at the Registry Office, and Peter and Chris had brought champagne and a camera. My red cartwheel hat I had bought from a charity shop, my flowery dress from Marks & Spencer. We booked the honeymoon suite at the Ashdown Park Hotel, a former nunnery in Ashdown Forest. We had a charming room overlooking the lawns descending to the lake. We went for a walk and a deer crossed our path. On returning we decided to have a bubble bath. I put in too much bubble mixture and Jay was bailing hard to prevent a flood. Dinner was superb with the chef providing us with tasty titbits between courses. At midnight, we were woken by the fire alarm and donned our white robes and matching slippers to congregate on the lawn. An orange moon hung low in the sky, and after twenty minutes we were told that the fire was a false alarm. After breakfast we had a swim in the deserted swimming pool and left for home. As it was the millennium we were given a commemorative plate and also a superb flower arrangement. We drank our champagne in the bubble bath yesterday. It was a wonderful one night honeymoon.

On Thursday, the weather was still warm and sunny, and about twenty people from the Art Society gathered to paint at Waystrode Manor. We took champagne, Sainsbury's celebratory cake, glasses and tablecloth and laid the table beside the lake. As people assembled for lunch they were puzzled, until I said 'My husband and I invite you for champagne and wedding cake'. There were gasps, laughter and clapping. One of our friends made a kind speech to end our impromptu reception. We had a formal family party later.

New love

Being married at our age meant that our children were mostly married with families. Jay's eldest son John is married to Carol. They have three children James, Andrew and Yasmin. The two boys are graduates and Yasmin is at university. Jay's daughter, Jane, subsequently married a Greek and Alex, his youngest son, subsequently died from cancer. He was most like Jay and we both miss him. The family were wary of me at first but have accepted me now, as they know I make their father happy.

Jay was seamlessly accepted by Fiona and Pete, who have two children Catherine and Christopher, both graduates. I think Fiona was relieved that now someone was looking after me. I sold my Tunbridge Wells house within twenty-four hours of it being on the market. I had recouped the money spent on the alterations, and sold it for more than the asking price to a lady moving from France. She had very little furniture, and was pleased to receive the items which I no longer needed. Jay had bought us a bungalow and we both shared the price. It has been ideal and we love it. It is opposite a wood with an apiary, surrounded by trees and within walking distance of town. We have built up the garden year by year, buying a plant on our wedding anniversary.

Our garden owes so much to Jay. He had always had the ambition to make a statue. He first drew a template to assess the dimensions, and then with stainless steel armatures moulded the terracotta clay into a figure, and then added the plaster to make the mould. He was very skilled, and now Aphrodite, made of cast stone, stands four feet five inches on her plinth, under the arch of purple clematis, cream jasmine and red roses, and backed by bamboo. She has an attractive face, with plaited hair and a faraway look in her eyes. She took two years to complete and was made on the patio. Jay had plenty of fresh air.

Jay also made a pond with a small waterfall. We have no fish as herons come looking for lunch, but we do have two frogs.

We have a room with glass on three sides which we call the garden room. Every morning as we silently eat breakfast we watch the birds. This morning a young thrush was enjoying a shower under the waterfall in the pond. We always read a poem at breakfast and we have our favourites, especially Dylan Thomas, Philip Larkin, Laurie Lee, Rupert Brook, John Betjeman and many others found in the excellent B.B.C. poetry series. We also have a studio in the garden where we both sit and paint our pictures.

Our days at home are enjoyable and we share the chores. The bungalow is so easy to clean, and often we wait until we are having a visitor before Jay does the vacuum cleaning.

We have mutual friends at the Art Society. Jay with his managerial experience was soon made chairman, making a few beneficial changes. We attended all the activities such as the portrait group where we took our turn as models, fully clothed of course. We attended the demonstrations, lectures, workshops and outdoor painting. There are art societies country wide who have portrait groups. It is a lovely Christmas present for a family to present them with a portrait. Some of our artists are really outstanding. We are so fortunate in having our own premises on the Pantiles in Tunbridge Wells. The Art Society has three major exhibitions a year and also private ones once you have been a member for three years.

I was anxious to show Jay my home city of Norwich and booked an hotel which surprisingly was the very place where I had lived as a pupil midwife, and where we ran our antenatal clinic. We went to Norwich Cathedral with its beautiful fan tracery ceiling. It was in this cathedral when I was aged four that I first heard Handel's Messiah, which I have loved ever since. The Norfolk School of Painting was made famous by such artists as Crome, Munnings; Cotman, Constable and Edward Seago, and many of the original paintings are now in galleries in Norwich Castle Museum. I so enjoyed showing them to Jay, and we now have a large print over our bed of a chestnut mare and foal by Alfred Munnings.

The Maddermarket Theatre with its apron stage is unique. When I was at school my French mistress often took part in the amateur plays performed monthly.

New love

Shakespearian plays, and plays by famous playwrights made it a great attraction and seats needed to be booked quickly, as it was a small theatre. The theatre is still very popular. We saw an Agatha Christie thriller, and Jay commented on the high standard, as we sipped our coffee in the courtyard in the interval.

I knew that Max Ellis, a previous neighbour of mine had bought a holiday home in Norfolk. I phoned him and he invited us to visit. He lived in a stylishly converted barn about five miles from Worsted. The village of Ruston was just a cluster of houses with a church and very difficult to find. Max had taught art and had been a good friend. He invited us to stay the following year. One of Max's interests is collecting bargains at sales and markets. He certainly has a good eye and the barn was most attractive. The large round oak dining table would always be surmounted with a spectacular flower arrangement. The sideboard in front of the window lit up the vivid collection of turquoise and amber glass. Max was very generous and every time we stayed would take us to his favourite places. There was the lifeboat restaurant in Cromer, overlooking the fishing boats and the crashing waves. Then, there was the library at Kelling, which was not a library at all, but a restaurant with a great selection of homemade cakes, a picture gallery, and a sale of old books and china. We would take a trip to see the seals sprawling on the sandy island at Blakeney, and we would be drenched with spray in our rowing boat. It has been wonderful to see Max and go to Norfolk most years. He has now sold the barn and lives in a lovely house in East Dereham.

When we arrived home after a trip to Norwich a letter was awaiting me from The Canterbury Oast Trust stating that Hamish, my autistic son with Asperger's syndrome, would have to leave. He had become very depressed and uncooperative. Lorna Wing had recently founded the Autistic Society and had originally diagnosed Hamish with autism, so I wrote to her asking for her advice. She advised that Hamish should only go to a unit specialising in autism. A professional worker at the farm spoke of a colleague who was setting up a new centre for the mentally disabled. His name was Richard Hollands. When he was asked if he would set up a unit specialising in autism he readily agreed and Hamish was his first resident. By then, Hamish was vomiting continuously with acute anxiety. Richard was ceaseless in his care, staying with Hamish until he slept. He arranged for Hamish to see a consultant psychiatrist at a private clinic where his medication was adjusted to his needs. Gradually Hamish improved and he eventually lived in a one bedroomed house in the grounds, the four houses being called Monteith Villas. Springs Community is at St Mary's Bay, situated in extensive grounds and facing the sea and Hamish was very settled there. He and Jay became fond of one another and Jay would always receive a card on father's day.

New love

In 2011, Social Services moved Hamish to a very unsuitable supported living unit where he was supposed to do his own shopping and cooking. The idea was for Hamish to achieve his full potential. After six weeks, support was withdrawn and eventually Hamish just bought pies or fish and chips. At the same time the G.P. withdrew the drug which should have given Hamish stability. Hamish's unit was over an hour's difficult journey so I had to deal with problems by phone. The four other residents had severe learning difficulties and the staff were underqualified to deal with someone with autism. They were kind but not funded to give Hamish the support he needed. It was obvious that Hamish was struggling but he never told us and never grumbled. Meanwhile both the G.P. and the social worker left and the psychiatric appointment made by the part-time G.P. did not materialise. The social worker had not replied to my appeal for help. In January 2012 Hamish had no social worker and a part-time G.P. The Autistic Society was a lifeline in giving me help and advice. Every time I rang social services I spoke to a different social worker and it was not until July that we were granted help by a conscientious Nigerian social worker, who was shocked at Hamish's condition and apologised for the lack of help received from social services. However, he left at the end of the month. In August, we had yet another social worker who has been very caring and efficient. By 2013, Hamish's vision was affected and he rapidly became blind. In February, he fell down the stairs and fractured his elbow and soon became incontinent.

He was admitted to the orthopaedic ward at Medway Maritime Hospital where his fracture was repaired. He also had a brain scan which revealed an inoperable brain tumour. Because of the lack of continuity of care and psychiatric help diagnosis was missed, although I had mentioned a tumour to the G.P. a year earlier. Hamish was so content on the orthopaedic ward where they looked after him so well and the food was excellent. He never realised his condition and said he was fine and never complained. By the end of May Hamish developed pneumonia and was transferred to the special care unit with twenty-four hour doctor coverage. He died peacefully on 2nd June 2013. I miss him but am thankful that he had such good care.

The day of the funeral was sunny. The U.R.C. minister was a friend of Fiona's and she was so empathetic and the service was beautiful. My grandson Christopher, spoke of his love for Uncle Hamish. As we sat in Fiona's garden after the service old school friends of Fiona's reminisced. (Hamish was never able to make close friends). One of Fiona's friends had travelled from Wales for the funeral, but most amazing of all was the presence of Richard Hollands, who had founded Springs Community and had retired to Malta. He had been so fond of Hamish who was the first resident, and he had built Monteith Villas named after Hamish.

Early in 2000 Jay had a phone call from his daughter Jane. She had decided to have a break. She is an arts graduate and producer of plays for the B.B.C. As she already spoke Greek she opted to work for a friend who was a Greek travel agent. Jane went to the Greek island of Tilos in the Dodecanese, so we decided to visit. Tilos is a small island, four hours by boat from Rhodes, but we travelled by hydrofoil only taking one and a half hours. Our attractive apartment was covered with flaming orange and magenta bougainvillea. There was a supermarket and a bakery. Signposted 'bacery'. One customer came in asking for Hovis causing great confusion. The village square had a cigarette kiosk looked after by an overweight man with Down's syndrome. The Greeks have a policy of giving simple jobs to injured servicemen, or those who are disadvantaged in some way.

Jane has a warm and outgoing personality and we were soon familiar with the geography of the rocky mountainous island. When the threat of marauding bandits was over people left the former capitol, on the side of a mountain, and near the castle, and now live in Livadia, in the valley. The roofless ruins of the old capitol are now inhabited by goats and a night club. The sea is warm and very stony underfoot, so we bought some spongy rubber shoes which were a mistake. The sea was buoyant and added to the shoes I found it impossible to put my feet to the ground. I was helpless with laughter as I tried in vain to reach the beach. I needed the help of two strong men as Jay was having the same difficulty. We had souvlaka at the tavern by the beach, and soon made friends with Nikko and his wife Bebe. We joined the trip to the ancient monastery, about twenty of us sitting on chairs and forms, all packed on the back of a truck. We would not have passed 'Health and Safety' rules. It was a hair raising experience as the truck ground its way up the winding mountainous road, with a sheer drop on one side. The monastery with its pretty terracotta tiles, dark wooden veranda and frescoed church was very beautiful. The next day Jane told us of a saint's day feast to be held on a mountain at the end of the bay. We arrived at eleven p.m. and entered the tiny whitewashed chapel with its icons and gaily decorated altar, where we were offered little batter cakes. We could hear the band playing and as we emerged we saw the bonfires and the barbecues dotted around, and by the light of the moon it appeared that the whole village was there. Presently, people arose and started dancing until there was a huge circle, the loud poignant Greek music from the band urging us on. I felt that I was taking part in some ancient ritual which had been celebrated for hundreds of years.

Jane had met a taverna owner, called Vasili, and they had fallen in love and eventually married. Although this was our first visit it was not to be the last.

When we stayed on Tilos we always flew to Rhodes. In times past the harbour entrance was bestraddled by a colossal statue of Atlas. Now there were two tall pillars surmounted by antlered deer. Mike Chaplin, the prestigious president of our art society organised a trip to Rhodes about five years ago and a dozen of us went. We would meet in the evenings to discuss our daily art work. We would then repair to the restaurant adjacent to the hotel and have a hilarious meal sitting at one large table. Rhodes is so paintable with its round Don Quixote windmills by the harbour, the castellated buildings and the cobbled streets where the Knights Templars had lived. There is a mosque, a minaret and the Palace of the Grand Master – renovated by Mussolini where he possibly thought it would be noble to make a resounding speech from one of the solid stone balconies. When we visited the seaside town of Lindos we were greeted by the honking of donkeys. Sometimes they carried a heavy load, including overweight people down the steep pathways. When the donkeys were released at night with their saddles removed they ran joyfully along without their owner and they knew their way home. When we reached home we started painting a picture of Rhodes for the next exhibition, as did others who had been to Rhodes, but they were all different. Although Jay and I paint the same scene we always interpret it differently.

Chapter ten

Realisation

His Banner over me was Love
The Song of Solomon, Anon

Jay had travelled widely in his work advising television companies worldwide while I hardly knew Europe. My first husband had a boat on the Thames and that was our holiday.

Jay had been reading an autobiography by the Italian sculptor, Benvenuto Cellini, written in 1558. He was intrigued with Cellini's description of the bronze statue of Perseus, holding the head of Medusa, which he had made with some difficulty. The statue was more than life size and Cellini had many problems. In his own words he says 'To add to the difficulties, the workshop caught fire and we were terrified that the roof might fall in on us'. He does have about ten apprentices helping! Later on he realised the bronze was not fluid enough and says 'I sent for all my pewter plates, bowls and salvers which numbered about two hundred', and he threw them in to join the bronze and all was well. The result was an amazing statue, perfectly cast except for one of the feet. Jay had seen the statue in Florence and was keen for me to see it. When we arrived in Florence the statue was

no longer on its plinth. We inquired at the Uffizi galleries
and we were told that the statue was being cleaned,
and we could see it in the building opposite. There was
no charge, and we walked along the scaffolding and
then the immense winged head of Perseus was before
us. We looked across to see the deadly head of Medusa
held aloft. When we glanced down, the strong muscular
body looked much larger because of its close proximity.
We were so privileged to be at such close quarters
to such a work of art. Cellini was one of the foremost
sculptors and goldsmiths of his day.

Us in Florence

We had queued at the Uffizi for two hours which could
have been avoided if we had bought tickets at the
door the day before. The pictures in our own National

Realisation

Gallery seem so clean and those in the Uffizi, apart
from Botticelli's Venus, seemed to rather lack lustre in
comparison. The Pitti Palace, in the terraced Bobolil
Gardens, had no queue and the pictures, works of art
and furniture were stunning, and worth seeing again.
There was so much to see in Florence and we could not
leave without viewing Michelangelo's David. Vasari had
written a contemporary account of the famous statue, in
a book written in 1568 of the 'Lives of the Artists' which
included Leonard do Vinci, Raphael, Titian, Botticelli and
many others. Vasari says of David 'The grace of this figure
and the serenity of its pose has never been surpassed'
and then he goes on to say 'To be sure, anyone who has
seen Michelangelo's David has no need to see anything
else by any other sculptor, living or dead'. We were not
disappointed when we entered the Accademia. David
was perfectly displayed on a plinth, in an alcove at the
end of the long hall. The concealed lighting enhanced the
beauty of the figure. I think Vasari was right.

We stayed in Florence for one week and then left for
the hill top villa of Grassina at Pelago. The villa was
sixteenth century, and we were given an immense key
to open our apartment and the ancient wooden door
groaned as we came into a stone floored and raftered
room, with more double doors to enter the bedroom.
We had a very pleasant stay, painting and swimming.
We made friends with three Norwegians who invited us
to a birthday party where we drank a delicious lemon
liqueur called limoniti and saying 'Skoal' at frequent
intervals as our glasses were refilled. The Norwegian's

Realisation

English was mainly learnt from the B.B.C. from programmes such as 'The Darling Buds of May' and they loved comedies such as 'Allo, Allo' and 'Hyacinth Bucket'. The next day, we piled into their car to go to the home farm to see olive oil being processed and to taste their wine. We met on the terrace, being regaled with delicious hors d'oeuvres. Then we were invited into a hall with a buffet. After this a joint of beef about three feet long appeared complete with sparklers! We hardly had room for a dessert. A one man band with all arms and legs in motion accompanied the dancing. It was amusing to see our Norwegian friends dancing the polka with great enthusiasm, with hands crossed behind their backs. On the way home we sang with gay abandon 'We'll meet again' and 'Land of Hope and Glory'. They said 'Oh! Yes, we always watch the last night of the proms'!

We love Italy. On a previous holiday we had visited Lucca with its wide and tall walls where Puccini had lived. There was a festival with very skilled flag waving by men dressed in multi-coloured velvet livery.

Another time we stayed at a farm outside Montecatini. The owner was an artist. Around the doorways vines were painted hanging with luscious black grapes. Every light switch was decorated with a delicately painted bird. Montecatini is a spa town and the spa building of white stone and arches was spectacular, with a pianist in tails playing Bach on a grand piano. It was surrounded by immaculate gardens, with beds of

Realisation

scarlet geraniums. In contrast, the old town, high on
a hill with its castle and cobbled streets, was popular
with artists and very picturesque.

Jay is keen on sculpture, so we visited Rome and I was
keen to see the old Roman city.

There is a Michelangelo statue in St Peters which is
so tender in the treatment of the faces and Vasari
calls it a Pieta. He says 'so wonderful that it staggers
belief that the hand of an artist could have executed
this inspired and admirable work so perfectly and in
so short a time'. It is in white marble and the tracery
of the veins and the delicacy of the sculpture earned
high praise for Michelangelo, especially amongst those
to whom he was financially dependent. The Borghese
Museum, in Rome, displaying Bernini's sculptures was
unforgettable. The detail of the hands dimpling the
thighs in the statue of Apollo and Daphne with leaves
sprouting from her outstretched fingers as she turned
into a laurel tree. It was all so unbelievably beautiful.

We stood overlooking the old Roman city, the pillars,
colonnades and temples, imagining it as a bustling city,
with statues of the gods prominently displayed, just like
the dictators of today. The coliseum made me shiver,
thinking of the animals below and the many good people
who had lost their lives for other people's entertainment,
and that now it was intended as a concert hall.

Realisation

Ben Brown in his book 'Angels and Archangels' has popularised Rome, and I thought this as I entered the Roman Pantheon, with its huge dome demonstrating the skill of Roman builders.

On another trip we flew to Venice Airport where a water taxi was waiting to take us to our hotel. It was quite misty and we passed mooring posts with no land in sight. Suddenly, through the mist, we saw as in a dream, the misty outlines of the Doge's Palace, and all took shape as we came nearer. It was a magical moment and I would suggest that this is the best way to approach Venice for the first time.

We had not realised that the first Sunday in September is the date of the Regatta and then we only heard by accident. It is not widely publicised. However, we booked seats on a small landing stage near the macchina, or the starting post, which was as large as a bandstand but square not round, draped in scarlet, with gilt pillars and festooned with flowers. The river was lined on each bank with families in boats, and all the balconies and windows were packed with people. It was a bit like the Lord Mayor's show but on the river.

Firstly, there was a procession of glorious carved wooden barges with figureheads of silver, prancing horses, golden mermaids, a crouching carved lion, and three leaping porpoises. This was followed by the golden barge, with red liveried trumpeters announcing its arrival. Then, came young men standing in their coloured boats – white, brown, yellow, green, mauve, red, pink and blue, and all the oarsmen's suits matched the colour of their boats. The women were in white with matching sashes, two to a boat. They looked like an Egyptian frieze. The gondoliers arrived, six to a gondola and there was great cheering from the banks. The organisers in the macchina steadily announced the races interspersed with music, and the atmosphere was electric. We were there for about three hours.

Venice is unique with no traffic, narrow streets and small wooden bridges. Around every corner there seems to be possible pictures to paint, or a church to explore. We went to a concert in the lofty cathedral-like church of the Frari. When we arrived for the evening concert there was a simultaneous gasp as the gilded and carved choir stalls were fully lit but the twenty foot high Titian painting, over the altar, glowed with the full glory of light, balance and colour.

The view from our hotel window overlooking a canal was always interesting. One day we saw a long boat approach heralded by the regular beating of a drum. Small children dressed in yellow life jackets were supposed to be rowing in time to the beat and they looked as though any time would do. I think they were canal 'Brownies'!

In the early eighteen hundreds, the church of La Pieta, on the waterfront, was a refuge for orphans and the babies were 'posted' at an opening in the wall. The

Realisation

priest at that time was the composer Vivaldi, also known as the red priest, because of his red hair. Vivaldi trained the young women to sing his often joyous compositions as a choir, and also as soloists who often became famous. We went to a concert at the Pieta where the musicians were dressed in period costume and played Vivaldi's 'Four Seasons'.

We were very fortunate with our second visit to Venice in choosing to stay in April, which coincided with St Mark's Day on 25th April. Our hotel was opposite the station, but overlooked the Grand Canal. I glanced out of the window and saw a very long boat with about eighteen rowers dressed in white. Crowds were gathering on the light stone bridge. A little later an ornate barge with musicians and an opera singer appeared, with a flotilla of the long boat and coloured gondolas, and the gondoliers in matching costume. It was a moving spectacle as they processed under the white bridge. As it was St Mark's day every woman was given a red rose. When we returned in the evening a young 'Romeo' popped up from behind the desk and gave me a beautiful red rose!

Jay's birthday is in January and very near to Christmas, and to avoid a party we arranged to have Christmas and New Year in Madeira. Our hotel was high on a hill overlooking the bay and very comfortable. The next day we explored Funchal and were impressed with the relaxed Christmas atmosphere. Soft music was playing Handel and Bach, a nativity scene was displayed in the high street complete with waterfall and life sized three kings in golden robes. A girls' school choir, in immaculate uniforms, were singing carols. Further along were life like farm animals standing amongst poinsettias. Father Christmas was driving his very realistic reindeers. The streets were not crowded with rushing shoppers buying last minute presents, very different from the U.K.

In the evening, all the glory of the Christmas lights was revealed. Above the Cathedral roof were ethereal looking angels made of tiny white lights. The palm trees with their cross patterned trunks were interlaced with coloured lights which also outlined the branches. All the streets had a different motif, such as poinsettias and even musical notation in lights strung across the street. Out to sea were small boats made of lights. It was all delightful, delicate and not overwhelming.

Christmas was celebrated quietly with plentiful good food. On Boxing Day dancers and singers with women in red and green traditional dress, and small black hats like upturned mushrooms, performed in the high street.

As Madeira usually has very little rain, previous generations had made gullies, or levadas, coming from the mountains tops to the valleys below to irrigate the bananas, being the main crop for export. It was very hard work and the Portuguese are a hardy people, being mainly short and sturdy.

Madeira is known for its abundant flowers displayed at the flower stalls, in the market, along the levadas and in the tropical gardens. Agapanthus line the country paths, poinsettias with their red leaves or petals form flowers as large as plates, and strelitzias, or birds of paradise with their orange petals, contrast with the peacock colours of their flowery 'beaks'.

On board the Santa Maria, Madeira

A statue of Columbus gazing out to sea is displayed in nearby gardens. He is fondly remembered as he married the governor's daughter in the fifteenth century. He is also remembered in the building of a fifteenth century replica boat, the Santa Maria on which we booked a trip. When we boarded, a red and green parrot was perched on my shoulder, and my photograph rapidly taken, as my laughing surprise is shown in the photo. The sailors had bare feet, baggy cotton trousers, and their heads wound in a bandana. It was fascinating to see them nimbly climbing the rigging, especially when the engines were silent and the sails unfurled. All was silent as the sails filled and billowed out, and we seemed to float along. All that could be heard was the swish of the waves and the creaking of the rigging. The boat was so small and it seemed incredible that a similar boat had crossed the Atlantic.

New Year's Eve in Madeira is very special. The harbour was full of cruise ships 'dressed overall'. Firework stations were strategically placed at intervals all around the bay and ready for midnight. After an excellent dinner we were given a bottle of champagne and directed to the roof. On the stroke of midnight the bay erupted into a display of fireworks of continuous intensity and wonderful patterns and colours. All the houses on the hillsides were lit as were all the cruise ships in the harbour. We drank our champagne in wonder and awe, wishing one another a 'Happy New Year' and we were moved to tears.

For every holiday we take our watercolours and paint small pictures of places we want to remember and perhaps to make into a large picture when we are at home. It is a marvellous way of fixing a view in one's mind. I also write a daily diary. In the winter it is cheering to read of warm holiday weather and other countries.

I look back on my long life, so much of which is about people who have been significant to me. My parents

Realisation

gave me the freedom to train as a nurse at a very fraught time in their lives.

Lois Beaulah, Matron of Queen Mary's Maternity Home gave me the foundation to be a good midwife.

Dear Anne Grafton of West Kensington Congregational Church, turned her personal tragedy into being a caring and loving woman, and she helped me in so many ways.

My first husband, Lionel Monteith, in advising me to have a personal analysis which gave me valuable insights into becoming more patient and understanding.

Fiona, my daughter, and Pete her husband have unreservedly seen me through some difficult times. Now I have the most wonderful partner and helpmate.

There have been so many people along the way who have appeared at a time of need, and many good friends.

Today the seventh of December, the day after the death of Nelson Mandela, I passed a sign outside a small restaurant which said 'Mandela. Thank you for your love. We shall never forget you'. I found this most moving. The important truth is love. Mandela was a man of compassion and reconciliation and this is what we shall remember.